How to write a CV
that *really!* works

D1004699

Visit our How To website at **www.howto.co.uk**

At **www.howto.co.uk** you can engage in conversation with our authors – all of whom have 'been there and done that' in their specialist fields. You can get access to special offers and additional content but most importantly you will be able to engage with, and become a part of, a wide and growing community of people just like yourself.

At **www.howto.co.uk** you'll be able to talk and share tips with people who have similar interests and are facing similar challenges in their lives. People who, just like you, have the desire to change their lives for the better – be it through moving to a new country, starting a new business, growing their own vegetables, or writing a novel.

At **www.howto.co.uk** you'll find the support and encouragement you need to help make your aspirations a reality.

You can go direct to **www.how-to-write-acv-that-really-works.co.uk** which is part of the main How To site.

How To Books strives to present authentic, inspiring, practical information in their books. Now, when you buy a title from **How To Books,** you get even more than just words on a page.

How to write a CV

really!

that works

REVISED AND UPDATED 4th EDITION

PAUL McGEE

howtobooks

Published by How To Books Ltd,
Spring Hill House, Spring Hill Road
Begbroke, Oxford OX5 1RX
Tel: (01865) 375794. Fax: (01865) 379162
info@howtobooks.co.uk
www.howtobooks.co.uk

Second edition 1997
Reprinted 2000
Reprinted 2001
Reprinted 2002 (twice)
Reprinted 2003
Third edition 2006
Reprinted 2007
Fourth edition 2009

ISBN 978 1 84528 377 3

British Library Cataloguing in Publication Data
A catalogue record for this book is available from the British Library

Cover design by Baseline Arts Ltd, Oxford
Produced for How To Books by Deer Park Productions, Tavistock, Devon
Typeset by PDQ Typesetting, Newcastle-under-Lyme, Staffs.
Printed and bound by Bell & Bain Ltd, Glasgow

Contents

List of Illustrations

Preface

There are not many certainties in life – death and taxes are probably the main ones. Now there is another. At some time, we are all likely to need a Curriculum Vitae, or CV for short. Whether we're leaving school or college, wanting a career change, experiencing redundancy or returning from a career break, our first priority is to get a CV written.

Not only is a CV necessary for the benefit of the intended reader, but as this book will illustrate, compiling one can provide a great insight for you personally. Rather than relying on someone who doesn't know you to write your 'personal sales brochure', this book gives you a practical step-by-step approach to creating your own.

We have all faced the frustration of knowing we can do the job, but how do we get 'a foot in the door'? Your CV is the key to opening those doors. You will learn not just how to sell yourself, but how to tailor and vary your approach accordingly. Interviews will also take on a new meaning when we see the role our CV typically plays in that situation. Packed with exercises and case studies, this book provides insights and tips gained from helping thousands of people of all ages and from all backgrounds to successfully market themselves.

In writing this book I would particularly like to thank my mum and brother Andy for all their support and encouragement over the years. I would also especially like to acknowledge, once again, my wife Helen. By her actions she continues to provide even more definitions to the meaning of the words partner and friend. Thank you.

As for my offspring, Matt and Ruth, the time is now fast approaching when you will need a CV. I hope for once you will value your Dad's advice!

Finally, I hope this book contributes in some way to the future success of all its readers. Good luck.

Paul McGee

Who Needs a CV Anyway?

LEARNING TO MARKET YOURSELF

Billions of pounds each year are spent by companies advertising their products. No matter how good the product is, no matter how well it has sold previously, businesses will continue to invest in its promotion. In America, television programmes are scheduled around commercials, and sporting events are delayed in order for the viewers to receive 'a message from our sponsor'.

A radio programme was examining factors that contribute towards a song being successful in the charts. There were a number of factors – but the most important was simply how well the song was marketed. Whether that came through television, on-line chatter or exposure via You Tube, success wasn't simply down to the quality of the song.

That's a lesson we could all learn from.

Strange as it may seem, people can also be viewed as products. When they apply for a job or sell their services, they sell their skills, experience, qualities and potential. No matter how good a 'product' the person is, their future success will depend to a great extent on how well they market themselves.

One of the most important marketing tools an individual can have when seeking to promote themselves is a Curriculum Vitae (CV for short) which is the Latin for 'the course of your life'.

WHO NEEDS A CV?

We live in a society where change is continuous and competition is increasing. The days of full employment are long gone and, whatever politicians say, they are unlikely to return. Advanced technology and emphasis on 'efficiency' has led to a reduction in the labour force. Economic realities mean:

◆ Many more women are being forced to return to paid employment in order to supplement their partner's wage.

◆ Companies are recruiting fewer graduates, which means there are plenty of qualified people, but with little or no work experience.

◆ A 'job for life' is becoming the exception rather than the norm.

◆ Reorganisations within companies have led to redundancies and people who have worked all their lives in one industry are now looking for alternative work for the first time.

◆ Increasingly there are more self employed people, working on short term projects.

◆ People must now be prepared to work on a temporary contract, without any job security.

◆ Working practices are changing and people are having to be more flexible in the hours they work. Whilst some are finding their home life is suffering due to the time spent at work, others are struggling to find even part-time employment.

These statements may seem stark, but this is reality and these are the circumstances people are finding themselves in.

The CV is not a magic wand. It will not suddenly be the solution to all our problems. But for those who do find themselves affected by this economic climate, or for those who simply feel it is time for a change, the CV is an important marketing tool.

Who needs a CV?

- School/college leavers
- Graduates
- Women returners
- Careers changers
- Those made redundant
- Consultants
- Writers (the publisher of this book wanted a copy of my CV)

When do we need a CV?

When applying for:

- Summer jobs
- Work placements
- Agency work
- Voluntary work
- Full and part time work
- Consultancy work
- Temporary work
- As an aid to filling in an application form

MAKING A CV WORK FOR YOU

The purpose of a CV is to inform briefly the reader of a number of points about yourself. This usually includes:

- personal details (name, address, telephone number)
- education
- training received
- work history – (the name of the company and how long you worked there)
- skills you possess.

Other details that may be included are:

- age and marital status
- addresses of where you worked
- hobbies and interests
- references.

The aim of a CV

However, the aim of the CV is to do more than simply inform the reader of your life to date.

My definition would be:

> **A CV is your sales document that highlights your skills, achievements and experience in such a way that the reader is motivated to meet you.**

The objective of a CV is **not** to get you a job or to win you a contract, but to get you an interview or meeting.

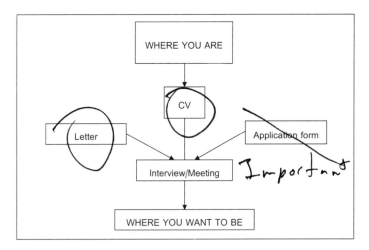

Fig. 1. The role of your CV in finding a job.

The CV plays a central role in getting you from where you are to where you want to be:

◆ It accompanies or helps in completion of an application form.
◆ It is usually accompanied by a letter.
◆ It leads to the all-important interview/meeting.

YOUR CHANCE TO 'SELL' NOT 'TELL'

I was looking to buy a house recently. When I visited estate agents, I collected a number of house details – in fact a great pile of them! The purpose of the details was to arouse my interest by:

◆ informing me of the particulars of the house
◆ presenting the property in the best possible light, so that I would want to view it.

I was not expected to look at the details and say 'I'll buy this house, please'. (Although I am sure the estate agents would not have complained if I had.)

Someone wanting to buy a house has a great number of properties to choose from. People may have certain criteria that need to be met:

◆ price
◆ location
◆ number of bedrooms
◆ size of garden.

But many houses may meet these criteria. The aim of the estate agent therefore is to present those details in the most attractive way, so that people want to visit the property to find out more.

Our CV must do the same. Whatever the purpose of the CV, our objective will not have been met unless it leads to a meeting. It is vital that we present ourselves in the best and most appropriate light. So our CV is not simply about supplying information about ourselves.

Our CV is our personal sales brochure

Unlike an application form, when we have little choice in what we include and the way we present the information, the CV is completely different:

- We design the layout of our CV.
- We decide what to include and what to exclude.
- We determine how long it will be and how it will be presented.

We are competing in an overcrowded market, seeking to grab the attention of our reader. Every day personnel managers, directors and managers are bombarded with literature, most of which will end up in the bin! A single job advert can result in a company receiving hundreds, if not thousands, of replies. So:

- How will we make ours stand out?
- How can we make an immediate, positive impact on the reader?

When we begin to see our CV as our personal sales brochure, which advertises what we **have done** and **can do** for the reader, then we have an increased chance of meeting our objectives.

Avoid information overload

Unfortunately, many people go straight into the 'tell mode'. A client who recently attended one of my courses had compiled a nine-page CV packed with information! The opening lines included:

- Age **and** date of birth (just to emphasise how old he really was!)
- All the schools and colleges he had attended throughout his life.
- The year he was married.
- The ages of his children.
- All his hobbies and interests.

This was followed by a detailed overview of his 35-year career! Sorry, but there was only one place this CV was going – in the bin.

When writing our CV, we should bear in mind the following:

It should be:
- Relevant
- Selling your achievements
- Easy to read and follow
- Detailed and accurate
- Truthful
- Highlighting the skills you have developed both in and outside of work.

It should NOT be:
- Full of irrelevant information
- A list of job titles and duties
- Jumbled and cramped
- Vague and lacking in detail
- Dishonest.

INVESTING SOME TIME IN SHAPING YOUR LIFE

This book then is written to equip you with the necessary insights required to market yourself. But it is not simply giving you information. You must play your part:

- **Think** about the questions asked.
- **Research** what you have done previously.
- **Analyse** the skills you have developed.

Why? Because this will help you know yourself better. It might help convince **you** that you have more to offer than you realised. The great British disease is modesty or feeling negative about ourselves.

Knowing yourself better

Many people could easily identify the good points in others, but find that hard to do about themselves. They feel uncomfortable. I am not encouraging you to be cocky and arrogant and tell the whole world how wonderful you are! I simply want us to look honestly and positively at:

- Who we are.
- What we have done.
- What we are capable of doing.

We take ourselves, our abilities, qualities, attributes and strengths for granted. In designing your own CV, I believe you will see that we are not simply going through the motions of an academic, one-off exercise, but something much more important. How you see yourself is vital. So many of us suffer from low self esteem and therefore fail to fulfil our potential. How we communicate ourselves to the outside world is also vitally important. A CV is just one way we do that. So work through this book and in doing so, invest some time in shaping your life.

ACTION AND REFLECTION

Action points

1 Write out your own definition of the purpose of a CV.

2 In what ways is a CV different from an application form?

3 List five uses for a CV.

4 What are the most common mistakes people make in compiling a CV?

5 Complete the sentence 'It is not how good the product is that determines its success, but . . .'

Points to consider

◆ How do you feel about having to sell yourself?

◆ Why is it that we find it difficult to feel good about ourselves?

◆ What motivated you to buy this book?

◆ Should CVs be written by ourselves or left to the so-called experts?

(2)

So What Have You Got to Sell?

THERE'S MORE TO YOU THAN MEETS THE EYE

Throughout my years working with people who are seeking alternative employment, I have often heard the following comments:

'I have only ever worked in ——. What else can I do?'

'I am only a housewife.'

'I will never get another job. There is no demand for what I do.'

'I don't have any qualifications, that's my biggest problem.'

'I know I can do the job, but I haven't got the experience.'

These comments are understandable and commonly heard. Which can you relate to? Can you think of any others?

A trap we often fall into is this:

We focus on our labels and not our skills.

or put another way:

**We concentrate on what we are called
rather than on what we can do.**

We tend to view ourselves in the following way:

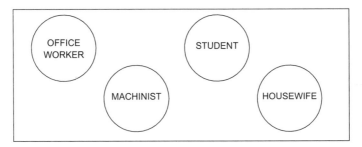

Fig. 2. The labels we give ourselves.

However, it is more helpful and constructive to view oneself as a person who possesses a wide range of skills in a number of areas, as Figure 3 illustrates.

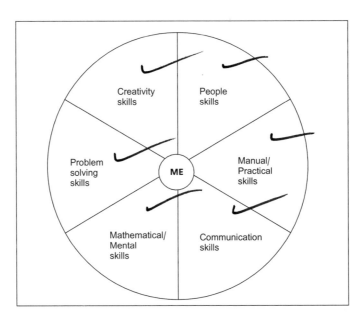

Fig. 3. How we should see ourselves.

We should see ourselves in this way and not with tunnel vision which may blind us to the wide range of opportunities that exist.

DOING A PERSONAL STOCK TAKE

The following exercise will help you to identify the skills you have which are readily transferable into other contexts. When completing this, please think about your abilities in both work and leisure activities. Many skills such as budgeting and organising may well have been developed 'in the home'. It does not matter whether you are paid for what you do; the important question is, do you believe you possess some skill in this area?

There are six categories to complete in this exercise. This is not exhaustive and you may wish to add further skills or categories.

1   Place a tick in the box if you consider yourself proficient in the area.

2   Write down an example which demonstrates your skill in that area.

EVALUATING YOUR PEOPLE SKILLS

Skill	Your example
☐ Listening to others	_____
☐ Encouraging others	_____
☐ Resolving conflict	_____
☐ Motivating people	_____
☐ Teaching/training others	_____
☐ Organising people	_____
☐ Any others	_____

EVALUATING YOUR MANUAL/PRACTICAL SKILLS

Skill   **Your example**

☐ Making repairs ✓   _____

☐ Building ✓   _____

☐ Taking measurements ✓   _____

☐ Maintaining equipment ✓   _____

☐ Operating machinery ✓   _____

☐ Using a computer ✓   _____

☐ Any others   _____

EVALUATING YOUR COMMUNICATION SKILLS

Skill   **Your example**

☐ Using the telephone ✓   _____

☐ Dealing assertively with people ✓   _____

☐ Story telling ✓   _____

☐ Public speaking/giving talks ✓   _____

☐ Talking to people in authority with
  confidence ✓   _____

☐ Writing letters ✓   _____

☐ Completing forms ✓   _____

☐ Any others   _____

EVALUATING YOUR MATHEMATICAL/MENTAL SKILLS

Skill   **Your example**

☐ Memorising figures ✓   _____

☐ Estimating ✓   _____

☐ Planning ✓   _____

☐ Making rapid calculations _____

☐ Judging distances _____

☐ Budgeting _____

☐ Keeping accounts _____

☐ Any others _____

ASSESSING YOUR PROBLEM SOLVING SKILLS

Skill   **Your example**

☐ Working out routes _____

☐ Crosswords (experiment) _____

☐ Coming up with new ideas _____

☐ Analysing alternatives _____

☐ Diagnosing faults or causes of problems _____

☐ Interpreting data _____

☐ Any others _____

EVALUATING YOUR CREATIVE SKILLS

Skill   **Your example**

☐ Creative writing _____

☐ Designing/decorating a room _____

☐ Finding alternative uses for things _____

☐ Craft making _____

☐ Musical _____

☐ Drama _____

☐ Improvising _____

☐ Cooking _____

☐ Using colours creatively _____

☐ Any others _____

Review the exercise you have done.

◆ Which categories had most ticks?

◆ Of all the skills you have, which would you include in your top 10?
List them below.

I am particularly skilled in:

1_____

2_____

3_____

4_____

5_____

6_____

7_____

8_____

9_____

10_____

Don't worry if you were not able to list 10 skills.

◆ If you can, ask someone you know to go through the exercise with
you. Do they identify skills you had not included?

◆ What are your reflections on doing this exercise? Any surprises?

IDENTIFYING YOUR ACHIEVEMENTS

Many people do not believe they have ever achieved anything in life!
As usual, people can tend to take for granted successes they have
had.

The following questions are designed to help you identify your achievements in three areas:

◆ work related
◆ leisure related
◆ home related.

Work related

1 What achievement during the last three to five years has given you most satisfaction?

_____

_____

_____

2 What skills and attributes did you demonstrate in order to achieve this?

_____

_____

_____

Leisure related

1 What achievement during the last three to five years has given you most satisfaction?

_____

_____

_____

2   What skills and attributes did you demonstrate in order to achieve this?

_____

_____

_____

Home related

1   What achievement during the last three to five years has given you most satisfaction?

_____

_____

_____

2   What skills and attributes did you demonstrate in order to achieve this?

_____

_____

_____

Again, you may find this exercise helpful if you were to enlist the help of someone who knows you well, for their input.

Often, before we are able to sell ourselves to the 'outside world', we need firstly to convince ourselves we have something to sell. So far we have identified two important areas:

- ◆ our transferable skills
- ◆ our recent achievements.

In the next chapter we will consider personal attributes and qualities as we develop a personal profile.

CASE STUDIES

Throughout this book, we will be following the experiences of four people who all require a CV. Here is an introduction to them.

Introducing Clare Griffiths

Clare is 37 years old and wants to return to work, having left banking eight years ago to start a family. Having conducted a personal stock take, Clare identified her main skills as follows:

- encouraging others
- resolving conflict
- teaching/training
- talking to others in authority
- letter writing
- budgeting.

Before the exercise, Clare had labelled herself as a housewife and mother. Her main fears were:

'I don't want to return to banking so what else can I do?'

'I have not worked for eight years, so what relevant skills have I to offer?'

The exercise showed Clare that a number of her main skills have been developed outside the work place, whilst raising two children and organising a busy household. She has also written to and met her local MP regarding the lack of child care facilities in the area.

The exercise also identified a training need in the area of word processing/basic computer skills.

Introducing Brian Lynch

Brian is 41 and has worked as a supervisor for British Coal for nine years. He joined the mine when he left school and has reached a senior position of colliery official. Brian identified his main skills as follows:

- ◆ motivating people
- ◆ making repairs
- ◆ dealing assertively with people
- ◆ talking to people in authority
- ◆ planning
- ◆ coming up with solutions or new ideas
- ◆ improvising.

Brian's main concerns were:

'Employers have negative perceptions of miners.'

'People do not appreciate the work done in a mine and the skills required.'

Brian realises it will be important to emphasise his managerial skills in his CV. If people have a stereotyped view of miners it will be important that Brian's CV communicates in a language they understand without constant reference to mining.

Introducing Joanne Taylor

Joanne is 22 and recently graduated from university. She worked in a large department store between school and university. Her degree was combined with a social work qualification; however, she now wishes to pursue a career in personnel management. Her main concerns were:

'Have I wasted the last four years because I don't want to go into social work?'

'I seem to lack business experience and commercial awareness.'

'Graduate jobs are scarce and I will be competing against those with more relevant degrees.'

Joanne identified her main skills as:

♦ public speaking
♦ talking to people in authority
♦ motivating others
♦ drama
♦ keeping accounts
♦ creative writing
♦ solving problems.

The exercise helped Joanne look beyond her course. Her placement as a probation officer gave her experience of dealing with a wide range of people, and her role as rowing club treasurer gave her experience of book keeping. She enjoys speaking to large groups of people, which she experienced during her involvement with the Student Union.

Her work experience before attending university also developed her maturity and was a taste of the commercial world. Joanne also admits to having a blinkered approach to her background, having a tendency to view things negatively and ignore the positive aspects.

Introducing Colin Burrows

Colin is 46 and a management accountant. He has just been made redundant after a company takeover. Colin has worked in accountancy since leaving school. He now wants a job outside accountancy.

Colin's concerns are:

'How many companies will even consider me at my age?'

'Will I be seen as "once an accountant always an accountant"?'

'I have always worked for larger companies, but it is the smaller ones that are now expanding. As a specialist in a particular field, will my experience within a large organisation be relevant to a small business?'

Colin completed the exercise and identified his main skills as follows:

◆ diagnosing faults or causes of problems
◆ planning
◆ organising people
◆ listening to others
◆ encouraging others
◆ dealing assertively with others
◆ setting up new systems and procedures
◆ budgeting.

As Colin is keen to find employment within an administrative function, he has highlighted an additional skill, 'setting up new systems and procedures'.

Colin now feels more confident that a career change is possible, but the key will be how well his CV communicates his experience and highlights the skills not normally attributed to those in accountancy.

ACTION AND REFLECTION

Action points

1 Focus on your skills and not your job titles.

2 Complete the exercise in identifying your skills.

3 Discuss your findings with someone who knows you well. How do they rate you?

4 Review your achievements in relation to work, leisure and the home. Which have given you most satisfaction overall?

5 Write down your skills and achievements on a piece of a card/paper, so you can refer to them quickly.

6 Are there any skill areas you would like to have been more proficient in? What steps can you take to improve these skills?

Points to consider

◆ How would you describe your attitude towards yourself and your future?

◆ Which would you consider more important – how others see you, or how you see yourself?

Have I Got News For You

Take advantage of this

The average length of time spent by someone reading your CV is a
staggering 20–30 seconds! The reader will quite often simply skim
through your CV in order to decide what happens next. One of three
things may happen:

◆ The reader will contact you to find out more.

◆ Your details will be kept on file.

◆ Your CV will be 'binned' and you may or may not receive an
acknowledgement.

REASONS FOR REJECTION

There are many reasons why your CV may not lead to an interview/
meeting. These include:

◆ The CV was never read by the intended person. *X Avoid*

◆ The CV was too long and boring and therefore was not read. *X Avoid*

◆ The CV was irrelevant to the reader's needs. *X Avoid*

◆ The CV was poorly presented on cheap paper, included spelling
mistakes and therefore did not deserve a positive reply. *X Avoid*

◆ The CV was difficult to follow because of poor layout and the
reader lost interest. *X Avoid*

◆ Your CV arrived too late to be considered. *X Avoid*

◆ The reader found your CV interesting but did not envisage any openings.

◆ Due to the volume of applicants your CV was never read.

Review the list and write down the reasons for rejection which we do not have control over:

_____

_____

_____

I believe that in the list outlined there are only two reasons why our CV is rejected that are beyond our control.

◆ The reader found your CV interesting but did not envisage any openings.

◆ Due to the volume of applicants, your CV was never read.

Throughout the book, we will see how positive action can counter the other reasons.

HOW TO SELL YOURSELF IN 30 SECONDS

If we have such a short time to hold the reader's attention, we need to make an immediate impact. As CV styles have developed, it has become increasingly common to include a profile.

**A profile is your banner headline –
a summary of your main selling points.**

Its aim is to:

- Give a brief overview of who you are.
- Highlight your main skills and experience.
- Communicate personal attributes.
- Motivate the reader to know more.

A profile sets the tone for the rest of the CV and helps precondition the reader.

An effective profile

There are no set rules about the length of a profile, but in order to meet the above aims, I suggest it should consist of between 30–50 words.

For example, you may see a job as a sales person which interests you. Your work to date has been in a bank, but you now want to make a change. The first part of your profile reads:

'A experienced **bank official** fully conversant with banking operations and procedures...'

You have already pigeon-holed yourself into one profession, one that seems to have no relevance to selling. However, if the first part of your profile read:

'An articulate and persuasive individual, who relishes challenges and working under pressure...'

You are using words that are relevant to the position applied for.

So the first few words of your profile are likely to determine whether the reader takes any more interest in your CV.

A profile must:

◆ be relevant

◆ be adapted accordingly

◆ contain positive statements that sell you. Remember first impressions count.

Below are a list of words you might wish to use in a profile. Circle those which you believe you could justifiably use to describe yourself.

Helpful words to use in your CV

Able ✓	Checking	Detecting
Accelerated ✓	Coaching	Determining
Accomplished ✓	Commitment	Developing
Accurate ✓	Communication	Devising
Achieved ✓	Compiling	Diagnosing
Acted	Completing	Diplomatic
Adaptable	Concise	Directing
Administered	Conducting	Discovery
Advanced	Conscientious ✓	Displaying
Advised	Consistent ✓	Driving
Analysed	Consolidating	Editing
Appointed	Constructive	Effective
Approachable	Consulting	Eliminating
Arranged	Contribution	Empathising
Articulate	Conversant	Empowering
Assembled	Co-ordinating	Enhance
Assessed	Counselling ✓	Ensure
Audited	Creative	Enterprising
Benefited	Cultivating ✓	Enthusiasm
Budgeted	Debating	Establishing
Built	Deciding	Examining
Capable	Defining	Exceeded
Caring	Delivering	Excelled
Challenging	Designing ✓	Experienced
Channelled	Detailing ✓	Expertise

Explaining
Expressing
Extended
Flexible
Forecasting
Founded
Fulfilled
Gained
Gathering
Geared
Guiding
Handling
Heading
Helping
Illustrating
Implementing
Improving
Improvising
Incentive
Increased
Influencing
Inform
Initiative
Inspecting
Inspiring
Instructing
Interpreting
Interviewing
Investigating
Judging
Keeping
Leading
Lecturing

Lifting
Listening
Learning
Maintaining
Managing
Manipulating
Mediating
Memorising
Monitoring
Motivated
Mounted
Negotiating
Notable
Operated
Organised
Oversaw
Persuasive
Phased
Piloted
Planned
Problem solving
Processed
Professional
Profitability
Projecting
Promoted
Provided
Qualified
Quantified
Repairing
Representing
Researching
Resolving

Resourceful
Responsible
Restoring
Satisfied
Selected
Setting goals
Significant
Skilful
Specialised
Stimulated
Stretched
Studied
Succeeded
Successfully
Superseded
Tact
Teaching
Team building
Tested
Trained
Trouble shooting
Tutoring
Uncovered
Understood
Upgraded
Utilised
Versatile
Widened
Won
Worked
Worth
Writing

Example profiles

–   An adaptable and enthusiastic individual who takes great pride
    in his/her work. Communicates well at all levels and is able to
    form working relationships quickly with a wide range of people.
    Possesses excellent administrative skills and is computer literate.

– An experienced supervisor who has developed good people/ management skills. Able to organise people and systems effectively in order to achieve objectives. Used to working under pressure and to meeting strict deadlines.

– A business graduate who has combined academic study alongside a successful placement with a major blue chip company. Gained experience managing and motivating others whilst directing student theatre production. Ambitious and enthusiastic, with a mature approach to life.

– As a mechanical engineer I have gained experience of both heavy and light industrial equipment, particularly in the area of hydraulics. HND qualified and willing to study further in order to progress my career. Comfortable communicating with senior management or on the shop floor.

– An accomplished and qualified business and management trainer, who quickly develops rapport with people. Dynamic and humorous approach helps create a stimulating learning environment. Maintains complete professionalism in all business matters.

– A conscientious and reliable sales assistant trained to NVQ level III. A friendly and positive approach to customers ensures good working relationships are established. Holds current first aid certificate.

Writing your profile

Refer back to your key skills, identified in the previous chapter. Now review the list of words circled in 'Helpful words to use in your CV.' Combine these and using the examples as a guide, write your own profile below. Write two versions:

- One aimed at a specific job or career.
- A general multi-purpose version.

First version

_____

_____

_____

_____

_____

Second version

_____

_____

_____

_____

_____

A CV does not necessarily require a personal profile and there are some instances when it may not be appropriate to have one:

- When applying to go on a course for further study. (Educational qualifications may be the most important criteria.)

- School leavers will find it difficult to sell skills and experience which they have yet to acquire.

- You may not feel comfortable having one.

Being confident in your profile

Profiles can provide an excellent summary of your skills and experience. But as we will see in Chapter 7, we need to be careful not to go 'over the top'. As it is only *our* opinion of ourselves, we must be able to justify the statements. It is also important that we use words we are comfortable with and understand. We do not want to give the impression that 'this person sounds too good to be true'.

PRESENTING YOUR CAREER HISTORY

When a person reads your career history, they want to know:

- ◆ What you have done.
- ◆ For how long.
- ◆ What you achieved.
- ◆ What skills you have developed.

However, when presenting a career history, common mistakes are to:

Include irrelevant information
(*eg* address of company worked for)

↓

Write a lengthy job description
(not what you achieved or what skills you developed)

↓

Use jargon
(which the reader does not understand)

↓

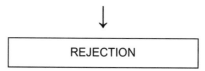

| REJECTION |

The inevitable consequence of the above factors.

Common questions

In Chapter 4 we examine the different styles we can use to present a career history. At this stage, we need to start gathering the facts. Before we do, let's deal with some common questions about our career history.

Q: How far do I have to go back?
A: This depends on your personal circumstances. The further back the job is, the less you need to write about it. The reader wants an overview of how long you've worked and your experience, but will be more interested specifically in what you have been doing in the last five to ten years.

Q: Some jobs I did only lasted a short time. Do I have to include all of them?
A: Again, this depends on your circumstances. If you are a school/ college leaver, then it may be appropriate to include summer and part-time jobs. This is not necessary if you have been employed for a lengthy period in a succession of permanent jobs.

Q: In the last two years I have worked for an agency in eight different companies. Some assignments lasted for three months, others for three days. How do I write that on my CV?
A: Rather than go into detail about every position, summarise your work, for example:

> '2004–2006 Jobwise Agency. Successfully worked on a number of projects ranging from administration to warehouse work.'

You could still highlight any particular achievements or skills developed during that period.

Q: I have been bringing up a family for the last seven years and therefore have not worked. How do I put that on my CV?

A: Although you have not been in paid employment, you have been working! Raising a family is no picnic. It will be helpful to analyse the skills you have developed during this period and for career history purposes write:

'1999–2006 Raising a young family and managing the running of a busy home.'

Achievements and skills

Now, starting with your current or most recent job, complete the exercises in Figures 4 and 5 (pages 33 and 34). The questions are asked in order to help you focus on your achievements and the skills used to do the job. Repeat the exercise for your previous positions if appropriate.

Having completed this exercise and written your profile, the bulk of your CV is done. What remains now is how to present your career history and this will be examined further in the next chapter.

DEALING WITH OR WITHOUT QUALIFICATIONS

If you have not gained any qualifications, this section can be quickly dealt with. Rather than draw attention to your lack of qualifications, simply miss out this section from your CV.

This is not something to be embarrassed about. Most graduates will tell you their biggest downfall can often be lack of work experience. If you don't have any qualifications, see this as an opportunity to expand further on your skills and experience.

Year   From _____ to _____

Name of company_____

Job title_____

Brief description of duties_____

_____

_____

_____

In what ways did the company expect to benefit from me doing that job?

_____

_____

_____

What would the consequence have been to the company if I had done the job wrong?_____

_____

_____

_____

_____

Fig. 4. Gathering information for your CV.

What skills did I use in this role in relation to:

People skills_____

_____

_____

Manual/practical skills_____

_____

_____

Communication skills_____

_____

_____

Mathematical/mental skills_____

_____

_____

Creative skills_____

_____

_____

Problem-solving skills_____

_____

_____

Fig. 5. Identifying specific skills.

For those who do have qualifications, we are already discovering that a CV is a very personal document. Its presentation and style will vary depending on the individual's circumstances and aspirations. How you present your qualifications will also vary; however, here are some points to consider:

- ◆ Always list your most advanced qualifications first. If you have a degree, this should be seen by the reader first, not your GCSE results.

- ◆ List all your subjects and grades only if this was required for the position, or if you are applying to go into further education. Otherwise, you can present the information in a brief form.

Example 1

You are applying for a job having spent eleven years in your previous position. Your qualifications are presented as follows:

1995 BA Hons degree in History from Nottingham University.
1992 2 'A' Levels in History and Geography.
1990 8 'O' Levels (including English and Maths).

Example 2

You are applying for a place to study for a diploma in business studies at a college of further education.

2001 Currently studying for 2 'A' levels in Economics and Information Technology.
1999 6 GCSEs in the following: Economics (B), Information Technology (B), Physics (C), English Language (C), Humanities (C), French (C).

The emphasis and space you give to your qualifications will therefore vary, depending on your objectives.

MAKING YOUR TRAINING CATCH THEIR EYE

Qualifications are not the whole story. The emergence of National Vocational Qualifications (NVQs) has placed more emphasis on a person's ability to do a given task, as opposed to sitting an exam. Training is then another necessary category to be addressed in a CV.

It is important to consider all the training you have received, but it might not be appropriate to include all this on your CV. Complete the exercise in Figure 6 as you consider the training you have completed. It is usual only to go back ten years; however, if you feel it would be relevant, include training that goes back further.

You are now in a position to include this information in your CV. However, beware of the following:

◆ Including too many courses attended. This can give the impression you spend all your time attending courses.

◆ Including training that is irrelevant to the job. This can hide more relevant information.

◆ Including training courses that happened too long ago to be still relevant, *eg* attended first aid course in 1963!

USING HOBBIES AND INTERESTS TO SELL YOURSELF

CV writers disagree about the benefits of including hobbies and interests in a CV. I would usually include them for the following reasons:

Subject	Qualification received (if any)	Additional information

Fig. 6. Recording your training.

Subject	Qualification received (if any)	Additional information
First Aid	Gained certificate from St Johns Ambulance	Certificate current + valid
Customer Care Course	No qualification available	Company in-house course
Word processing and basic IT skills	Gained distinction in passing both exams	Nothing to add

Fig. 7. Example of a training record.

- They form a basis for discussion at the interview.
- They help paint the 'whole' picture of you.
- They can highlight skills developed outside the workplace.

The interviewers will have two objectives when meeting you. They need to satisfy the following criteria:

- Will this person fit in?
- Can this person do the job?

'Can the person do the job?' can normally be gained by assessing the person's skills and experience to date.

However, the question 'Will they fit in?' is harder to answer. Hobbies and interests provide a clue. We will take a closer look at the role of the CV at the interview in Chapter 7.

What are your interests?

Many people can be put off by the term 'hobby', so an easier way of dealing with this is to answer the following questions:

1 What do I enjoy doing in my spare time?

_____

_____

2 What sports do I participate in or watch?

_____

_____

3   Am I a member of any clubs or committees?

_____

_____

4   Am I developing any particular skill or interest at a college or
    night school?

_____

_____

5   What did I do last weekend? What will I do this weekend?

_____

_____

6   What do I like to do on my own?

_____

_____

7   What do I like to do with others?

_____

_____

You should now have enough information for this section of your
CV. Beware of the following:

♦   Including too many interests. (When does this person have time
    to work?)

♦   Lying about hobbies in order to sound impressive (*eg* 'avid opera
    goer' – you saw Pavarotti once on TV).

♦   Including inappropriate interests. (This depends on what we call
    inappropriate, but I have seen CVs that included witchcraft and
    euthanasia amongst a person's interests!)

What do they say about you?

Below are some examples of leisure interests and the beneficial insights that may be drawn from them. Remember – as far as is possible, the emphasis in a CV is always on selling yourself.

Interest	Benefit
Swimming	This person keeps fit.
Fishing club treasurer	They can be trusted and are able to accept responsibility.
Using computers	With the importance of information technology at work, this is always useful.
Socialising with friends	This person is likely to be a team player as opposed to a loner.

Not all interests can be seen as having a definite benefit linked to them; however, you will find the following exercise useful to complete. Consider what impressions the reader is likely to gain from your interests.

Interest	Possible impression created
_____	_____
_____	_____
_____	_____
_____	_____
_____	_____

PUTTING ACROSS PERSONAL DETAILS

Where this section should appear on your CV is examined in the next chapter. But what should be included? This is up to you – remember there is no perfect way of presenting your CV. It is your personal sales brochure, so you decide. Here are some guidelines.

Essential to include

♦ Name
♦ Address
♦ Telephone number

Probably include

♦ Marital status
♦ Date of birth

Optional to include

♦ State of health
♦ Number and ages of children
♦ Nationality

A lot of things can be 'read' into your personal circumstances which may or may not be to your advantage, depending on the attitude of the reader.

For example:

♦ 'Married with children' – Probably lives in a stable environment. Needs to work to provide for family.

♦ 'Divorced no children' – No ties. Likely to be flexible and mobile. Can commit themselves fully to the job.

So rather than worry about what to include and the impression that may be created, keep this section brief and expand on any issues at the interview if need be.

USING REFERENCES

The inclusion of references is optional.

Advantages

- You may be able to include a well respected and well known individual who would impress the reader.

- The reader can contact a referee immediately to 'check you out'.

- If you have not been in paid employment, references may lend weight to your case.

Disadvantages

- References may be seen as irrelevant at this stage of the application.

- They use up valuable space on your CV.

- They may need to be changed frequently, depending on the job you apply for.

- If you are not able to include your current employer they may lack some credibility.

CASE STUDIES

Colin Burrows reaches a decision

Colin has written his profile and identified his key skills and achievements.

Profile

A qualified management accountant, FCMA and experienced financial/secretarial administrator in both large and medium sized companies. Experienced in meeting strict deadlines through effective communication skills and personal commitment to the job.

Comments

Colin's profile reflects his experience in accounting and as a financial/secretarial administrator. Colin wanted to move away from accountancy, but needed to review his options. Before doing so, he had to consider the following:

◆ Am I prepared to retrain?

◆ At my age, can I afford to make a career change?

◆ Am I prepared to join a company at a significantly lower level than my previous one in the hope of working my way up? (Colin could not expect to make a career change and yet stay in the same position as he had within his accountancy roles.)

Colin has therefore decided to stay in the accountancy/financial sector and his profile reflects this. It also demonstrates that:

◆ He has achieved success in his career to date, being a qualified management accountant.

◆ He has experience in medium and large size businesses. (This may be an issue if Colin applies to smaller companies and one he must be prepared to address.)

◆ He is able to work to deadlines and is an effective communicator who brings personal commitment to a job.

Colin's profile contains specific information that would be of interest to certain sectors, *ie* his accountancy and administration background. The inclusion of the initial FCMA also assumes the reader is familiar with such terminology.

Brian Lynch identifies his skills

Brian has identified his key skills and presented them as follows:

Key skills

◆ Managing and supervising 50 staff on a regular basis and up to 200 on occasions.

◆ Liaising and consulting with senior management on matters relating to productivity and safe working practices.

◆ Motivating and inspiring colleagues to achieve optimum productivity whilst working to strict deadlines.

◆ Implementing health and safety regulations.

◆ Organising the development of staff over a three-shift system and being accountable for both productivity and work standards.

◆ Checking the performance and suitability of safety equipment.

Comments

This is an excellent example of selling your skills, not just a job title. Reading these skills alone, it would be difficult to identify the industry Brian had worked in. This is exactly Brian's aim, as he seeks to demonstrate skills that would be relevant in a number of different industries. As we will see, though, in Chapter 7, it is important that Brian can justify and expand on these points further at the interview. Statements such as 'motivating and inspiring colleagues...' and 'organising the deployment of staff' are bound to elicit the response from the interviewer '...and how did you do that?'

Clare Griffiths compiles a profile

Clare has now compiled a profile.

Profile

A well organised individual, used to working under pressure. Communicates well both in writing and orally and enjoys working with a wide range of people. Self motivated, with an outgoing personality and the determination to succeed.

Comments

This is a general profile that is not targeted to one specific area. It summarises Clare's personal attributes briefly, but does not indicate what experience Clare has. It will be important that the rest of the CV adds weight to the profile with some substance regarding her experience and achievements. Clare's personal qualities do, however, have relevance to a wide range of jobs, where communication, organisation and the ability to work with people are necessary. Clare's attributes, if they can be backed up, would be of interest to most readers.

ACTION AND REFLECTION

Action points

1 Purchase some quality A4 paper (85 gsm minimum).
2 Whichever layout you decide on, make your sure your CV is clear and easy to read.
3 Compile your personal profile – a summary of your main selling points.

4 Complete your career history exercise and identify your skills and achievements.

5 Assess which of your hobbies and interests to include in your CV.

6 Identify any training courses completed and locate relevant certificates if applicable.

7 Consider whom to approach to act as a referee if required.

Points to consider

◆ How comfortable do you feel talking about your achievements?

◆ What factors contribute to whether or not it is wise for you to make a career change?

(4)

There's More Than One Way to Present Yourself

So far, we have been analysing why it is so important to 'sell yourself'. We have examined how to identify your skills and achievements and what information to include on your CV. This chapter concentrates on how to present this to the reader.

PUTTING ON THE STYLE – WHICH APPROACH TO TAKE

There are three main styles of CV:

1 The chronological CV.
2 The functional CV.
3 The targeted CV.

Each one has its strengths and which style you use will depend on:

◆ what you have already done
◆ what you intend to do.

It may well be appropriate for you to have more than one version of your CV (in most cases it is) and to present yourself using different styles. Let's examine each one in more detail.

The chronological CV

This style of CV presents your career history in chronological sequence, starting with your most recent job first. This style is useful when:

♦ Your career history shows natural progression and growth.

♦ You're staying in the same field of work.

♦ You have worked for well known companies with good reputations.

♦ Your previous job titles are impressive.

♦ You're aiming to work in a traditional field, *eg* government or education, when where you worked or studied is important.

Your last or current position should include more information about your duties, skills and achievements than previous ones. In most cases, the less recent your job, the less information you will include. Remember, when writing about your work, only include:

♦ the main highlights
♦ what you achieved (not just what you did)
♦ the skills you developed
♦ facts and figures that help sell you (*eg* managed a team of 14 staff, working to a budget of £250k).

So if your career to date emphasises continuity and progression and you have worked for well known employers, this style may well be best for you.

The functional CV

This style of CV highlights your main skills and strengths and does not place so much emphasis on who you worked for and what your job title was. The functional CV offers greater flexibility on how you present yourself than a chronological CV.

This style is useful when:

◆ You want to emphasise skills and strengths not necessarily acquired through paid employment.

◆ Your career to date consists of a number of jobs, most of which are unconnected.

◆ You want to change careers and therefore your present position may be of no relevance to your future ambitions.

◆ You want to emphasise skills and achievements from previous work experience which were not required in your most recent position.

◆ You are entering the jobs market after a break or for the first time.

◆ Most of your work has been freelance or you have worked on a number of temporary assignments.

◆ You are self employed and want to present to clients the range of areas in which you have experience.

◆ You have had a number of job titles, but the work has been basically the same. (Using this style avoids endless repetition of the same information.)

This style can be used when sending your CV on a speculative basis, (we look at this in more detail in Chapter 6) as it gives a brief overview of the range of your skills, rather than simply emphasising what you have done in your most recent position. For this reason it is also useful when contacting agencies who may wish to consider you for a number of positions.

The targeted CV

This style of CV, as the title suggests, is best to use when you are aiming for one specific type of job. As such, the CV can only be written with the job in mind. Although much of the content of the CV may be the same as used in the previous styles, this one will be tailored accordingly. Greater emphasis will be given to detail that relates **specifically** to the job in question.

A targeted CV can be a combination of functional and chronological CVs. However, all detail included will be written with a clear objective in mind, as opposed to a general overview.

This style is useful when:

◆ You have a specific job to go for, or are responding to a particular job advert.

◆ You want to emphasise skills and achievements, not necessarily acquired in your most recent work, or which were obtained outside paid employment.

Adopting this style will, by its nature, mean you are likely to have a number of versions of your CV which you adapt accordingly.

GETTING THE LENGTH AND LAYOUT RIGHT

One of the main talking points around CVs is how long they should be. It is helpful firstly to answer the following:

◆ Does my CV give enough information to the reader?
◆ Have I been able to portray fully my skills and achievements?
◆ Am I getting interviews?

The third question is perhaps the most vital one. Ultimately, if you are not gaining interviews:

◆ you are applying for the wrong types of jobs
◆ your CV needs changing
◆ you need to adopt different strategies for using your CV. (We examine this further in Chapter 6.)

It is difficult, in my opinion, to say categorically how long your CV should be. The readers of your CV have different preferences. However, here are some guidelines from my experience.

Most people agree that there is no need for a CV to be any longer than three pages – and quite often two pages is enough. To some extent, this will depend on the size of type face and how spread out your information is. There are those that argue that a one-page CV proves most successful and that it should be possible to include all relevant information on one page. Certainly, if the reader is inundated with CVs and only has to glance through one page of yours, this may be an advantage. However, I have seen no evidence to suggest that someone is more likely to succeed with a job application if they have a one-page CV as opposed to a two- or three-page one.

Those are some general guidelines, although I am sure you will find some recruiter somewhere who is a fan of the six-page CV. The key, I believe, is to concentrate on what you want to tell the reader and then decide how long your CV will be.

MAKING FIRST IMPRESSIONS COUNT

The length of your CV will depend on how you decide to lay out your information and also on which one of the three styles you choose to use. When someone sees your CV for the first time, they will begin to form a strong impression immediately. This will be influenced by:

+ the quality of paper used
+ how neatly the CV is presented
+ whether or not the CV is clear and easy to read.

The reader does not want:

+ eye strain from trying to decipher a mass of words crammed onto a single sheet of paper

+ to be faced with a seemingly never-ending document that fails to get to the point and does not give them the information they require.

Remember:

> **Your CV must look good visually and be easy to follow.**

So the use of headings, bullet points and bold lettering can all play their part in helping to achieve this.

EXAMPLE CVs

Let's examine how an individual's CV can be presented using the three approaches discussed previously.

Paul Hughes works for Headway Consultants as a Trainer and Consultant. Figures 8, 9 and 10 show the three different ways of presenting his skills and experience. In Figure 10, the targeted CV, Paul has seen a specific job for a training consultant working with a consultancy which specialises in the financial sector.

Paul Hughes
33 Martha Road
Bridgnorth
Kent
ME12 5JL
(01822) 94177

Profile
A highly experienced Trainer/Consultant with excellent communication and analytical skills.

Career History

2004 – Present   Headway Consultants
- Work successfully as part of a team providing a full range of training and consultancy services to mainly Blue Chip organisations.
- Design and deliver courses including Recruitment and Selection, Managing Change, Total Quality Management and General Management Training.
- Manage a number of projects from conception to completion, working to budgets of up to £400K and with up to 8 consultants.

1996 – 2004   Arpley Foods Ltd
Progressed to position of Assistant Personnel Manager in a factory employing 650 staff. My hands-on role involved all aspects of human resource management from recruitment through to redundancy. Introduced an Absenteeism Review Panel which led to a 20% reduction in absenteeism levels within a year. Negotiated new working practices with the Trade Union which led to a 12% increase in production and a manpower reduction of 5%.

Fig. 8. Example of a chronological CV. (continued overleaf)

| 1994 – 1996 | CPF Insurance Services |
| | Worked in the claims department analysing and assessing client claims. Liaised between management and outside agencies. |

Education/Qualifications

1991 – 1994	Bradford University – BA (Hons) in Politics and Economics.
1991	Bury Grammar School – 3 'A' Levels in Economics, Politics and History.
1989	9 'O' Levels (including Maths and English).

Training ?

2004 – Present	Have received ongoing training with Headway Consultants Ltd in relation to customer care, personal development and strategic management.
2004	Gained Diploma in Training and Development (ITD).
1998	Attained my IPM qualification through open learning.
1998	Completed in-house Management Development programme with Arpley Foods Ltd.
1997	Interview and Selection Course with Saville and Holdsworth.

Membership of Professional Bodies
Institute of Personnel and Development (IPD)

Personal Details

| Status: | Married |
| Date of Birth: | 4th April 1973 |

X

Interests
Rugby, Tennis and Painting — maybe

Fig. 8. Continued

Paul Hughes
33 Martha Road
Bridgnorth
Kent
ME12 5JL
(01822) 94177

Profile
A highly experienced manager with extensive experience gained from a background in Human Resource Development

Key Skills and Achievements
Man Management/Interpersonal Skills
- Held a senior management position for a company employing 650 staff.
- Developed excellent communication and motivational skills in successfully managing a team of 8 consultants in achieving objectives and implementing training solutions for Blue Chip organisations.
- Conducted in depth negotiations with union officials in order to increase company profitability through greater efficiency. Demonstrated tact and diplomacy, coupled with an ability to remain calm under pressure, in order to achieve a positive outcome.

Training Development
- Design management and personal development courses for middle to senior managers.
- Deliver training packages to groups ranging from 6 to 60 people.
- Conduct training needs analysis and skills audit for medium to large businesses.
- Work on a one to one basis with senior managers, coaching for improved performance.

Human Resource Development
- Organised the recruitment of 150 temporary staff for Arpley Foods from an initial application of over 2000.
- Implemented an Absenteeism Review Panel which led to a 20% reduction in absenteeism levels within one year.
- Developed amicable working relations with Union officials in order to achieve successful and swift outcomes on IR matters.

Fig. 9. Example of a functional CV.

Career History

2004 – Present	Headway Consultants Ltd
1996 – 2004	Arpley Goods Ltd
1994 – 1996	CPF Insurance Services

Education/Qualifications

1991 – 1994	Bradford University – BA (Hons) in Politics and Economics
1991	Bury Grammar School – 3 'A' Levels in Economics, Politics and History
1989	9 'O' Levels (including Maths and English)

Training

2004 – Present	Have received ongoing training with Headway Consultants Ltd in relation to customer care, personal development and strategic management.
2004	Gained Diploma in Training and Development (ITD).
1998	Attained my IPM qualification through open learning.
1998	Completed in-house Management Development programme with Arpley Foods Ltd.
1997	Interview and Selection Course with Saville and Holdsworth.

Membership of Professional Bodies

Institute of Personnel and Development (IPD)

Personal Details

Status: Married   Date of Birth: 4th April 1973

Interests

Rugby, Tennis and Painting

Fig. 9. Continued.

Paul Hughes
33 Martha Road
Bridgnorth
Kent
ME12 5JL
(01822) 94177

Profile

A successful TRAINING CONSULTANT with extensive experience in working within the finance sector. Gained 1 year's experience in insurance before developing a progressive career in Human Resource Development. Design and deliver training solutions in order to meet client objectives.

Achievements

◆ Successfully implemented a Management Appraisal Scheme for a large insurance company employing 800 staff.
◆ Trained 30 senior bank managers in 'Powerful Presentation Techniques' and 'Successfully Dealing with the Media'.
◆ Presented a seminar on 'Managing in the 1990s' at the Royal Institute of Chartered Accountants Conference 1993.

Career Progression

Headway Consultants Ltd   2004 – Present

◆ Work successfully as part of a team of training consultants providing a range of consultancy services to mainly Blue Chip organisations.
◆ Design and deliver training courses, including 'Sales and Marketing in the 90s', 'Customer Care' and a wide range of management topics.
◆ Manages a number of key accounts overseeing projects from conception to completion, working to budgets of up to £400k and with a team of up to 8 consultants.

Arpley Foods Ltd   1996–2004

◆ Progressed to position of Assistant Personnel Manager within an organisation employing 650 staff.
◆ Covered all aspects of the function from recruitment to redundancy.
◆ Successfully introduced an Absenteeism Review Panel, which led to a 20% reduction in absenteeism levels within a year.
◆ Negotiated new working practices with Union officials, which led to a 12% increase in production and a manpower reduction of 5%.

Fig. 10. Example of a targeted CV.

| CPF Insurance Services | 1994 – 1996 |

♦ Worked in busy claims department, handling over 1000 claims daily. Involved in assessment and recommendation, frequent contact with senior management and outside agencies.

Education/Qualifications

1991 – 1994	Bradford University – BA (Hons) in Politics and Economics
1991	Bury Grammar School – 3 'A' Levels in Economics, Politics and History
1989	9 'O' Levels (including Maths and English)

Training

2004 – Present	Have received ongoing training with Headway Consultants Ltd in relation to customer care, personal development and strategic management.
2004	Gained Diploma in Training and Development (ITD).
1998	Attained my IPM qualification through open learning.
1998	Completed in-house Management Development programme with Arpley Foods Ltd.
1997	Interview and Selection Course with Saville and Holdsworth.

Membership of Professional Bodies

Institute of Personnel and Development (IPD)

Personal Details

Status: Married   Date of Birth: 4th April 1973

Interests

Rugby, Tennis and Painting

Fig. 10. Continued.

GIVING THE READER WHAT THEY WANT TO READ

Having looked at those three examples, it is important to realise that one is not necessarily better than any other. It depends on the job applied for and what the writer's objectives were. Each version needs to be right for the particular situation.

Therefore tailor your CV accordingly. Place greater emphasis on what the reader wants to know and less emphasis on irrelevant areas.

> **Having more than one version of your CV means you are able to present yourself in the best and most appropriate light.**

Whichever style you prefer, always remember your aim is to:

Give the reader what they want to read.

Paul Hughes' targeted CV emphasises information and experience relevant to that particular job, *ie* his training experience in the financial sector. That CV is right for that job, but it may be inappropriate for other positions.

The key is to remember that, no matter how right you may be for a particular position, it is how your CV portrays you that counts.

For that reason, we must be prepared to adapt our CV continually, even if that adaptation only requires minor changes.

Note that the second part of Paul's CV, from 'Education and Qualifications', remained the same in each version.

CASE STUDIES

Colin Burrows' CV

CURRICULUM VITAE
Colin Burrows
22 Leeming Way
Vale Park
Warrington
Cheshire
WA9 2PF
Tel: (01925) 444900

Profile

A qualified Management Accountant, FCMA and experienced Financial/Secretarial Administrator both in large and medium sized companies. Experienced in meeting strict deadlines through effective communication skills and personal commitment to the job.

Key Skills and Achievements

Financial and Management Accounting: Effectively managed day to day control of Finance Department to strict Accounting deadlines. Fixed Assets reporting in excess of £25m. VAT liaison officer. Department Budgets and Forecasts with variance reviews, including Central Distribution costing control.

Computerised Accounting Systems/Electronic Banking:
Controlled batch and on-line systems output, mainframe: IBM, HP, ICL, MSA, Micro: knowledge of Lotus 123 and Supercalc. Introduced and controlled electronic banking – Reuters.

Staff/Supervisory Control: Substantial man management experience, from 4 to 21 staff, including part and qualified personnel. Interviewing, appraising and job evaluation.

Cash Management and Credit Control/Sales Ledger: Cash Flow – Forecasting/Payment and Receivables – FX deals, SWAPS and FRAs Negotiations with Bankers. Reducing Credit days in one company from 54 to 35 days.

UK and US Dollar Accounting: Preparation and control of Period Management Accounts. Annual Company Accounts and Tax Computations, prior to audit.

Communications/Reporting: Presentations to both senior and junior personnel. Reporting to other disciplines, DP Manufacturing, Marketing, Sales etc.

Company Administration: Liaison with Bankers, Insurers and Solicitors. Attendance at Board Meetings, Report Writing.

CAREER SUMMARY

2001 – 2006	**M6 Cash and Carry, Haydock**
	Management Accountant
1995 – 2001	**Macro SS Wholesalers, Manchester**
	Financial Accountant
1993 – 1995	**British Telecom, Oxford, ICL, Stevenage**
	Contract Accountant
1989 – 1993	**Levi Strauss (UK)**
	UK Financial Accountant
1985 – 1989	**Westbrick Products, Leicester**
	Accountant/Company Secretary

1982 – 1985	**Messenger & Co, Loughborough**
	Company Accountant
1980 – 1982	**ICMA Sandwich Course**
	Derby College
1978 – 1980	**Redland Group, Leicester**
	Commercial Trainee

Education and Training

Hinckley Grammar School

ONC Business Studies 1978

FCMA 1992

Company Seminars including: 'Managing for Productivity', 'The Successful Manager', HAY/MSL Job Evaluation', VAT & Accountancy updates.

Personal Details

DOB: 12 November 1960

Marital Status: Married with 2 children

I hold a full clean driving licence

Interests

Badminton, walking. Leader of the local Youth Club. Baptist Church Member. Volunteer helper at Night Shelter for homeless.

Comments

Colin's CV contains plenty of information, yet comfortably fits into two sides. It is easy to read, which is helped by using bold lettering.

This CV is ideal now that Colin has decided to stay in accountancy and, therefore, it is acceptable to include jargon/terminology specific to that field.

Colin's interests also show there is more to him than just work and indicates that he likes to keep fit and be involved in the community.

Perhaps a minor point is the use of the title Curriculum Vitae in bold type at the top of the page. It takes up valuable space and it is fairly obvious to the reader what the document is.

Overall, this CV does a good job selling Colin's skills and experience, although it does not emphasise his personal qualities and attributes.

Clare Griffiths' CV

Name:	Clare Griffiths	**Date of Birth:**	15/8/69
Address:	14 Bronwich Close	**Status:**	Married
	Stockton Heath		2 children
	Warrington		
	Cheshire	**Health:**	Excellent
	WA4 2FL		

Telephone: (01925) 333335

Profile

A well organised individual used to working under pressure. Communicates well, both written and orally and enjoys working with a wide range of people. Self motivated with an outgoing personality and the determination to succeed.

Key Skills and Achievements

◆ Responsible for an annual household budget exceeding £15000.

◆ Parent governor of a school with over 250 pupils.

◆ Utilised tact, diplomacy and a determined attitude in order to achieve the establishing of further child care facilities in the locality.

◆ Works well under pressure and to tight deadlines.

◆ Able to motivate and organise others in order to achieve objectives.

◆ Runner up in the Bank Employee of the Year award in 1993.

Career History

1985 – 1998   Barclays Bank Plc.

1989 – 1998   Senior Personnel Assistant (Staff Accounts)
Authorised all staff borrowing in the Bank, which included personal loans and overdraft requests within discretions up to £35000. Deputised in Personnel Administrator's absence and acted as a point of contact for all managers and staff throughout the Bank (circa 4500 staff) on staff account issues.

1985 – 1989   Payroll Clerk
Updated and maintained employee records via manual and PC systems and provided payroll assistance to Bank staff. Covered all payroll procedures including SMP, SSP, PAYE and the executive payroll. Achieved weekly/monthly payroll deadlines.

Education

1979 – 1985   Appleton Grammar School.

7 'O' levels (including Maths and English)

Training

Currently studying RSA Stage 1 Word Processing.

Hobbies/Interests

Keep fit, School Parent Governor, Camping with family

Comments

Despite not working in paid employment for eight years, Clare has been able to demonstrate up-to-date skills and achievements, including the managing of a £15000 a year household budget. She also gives a good overview of her banking experience. Although she does not want to return to this field, she does not dismiss the experience gained, which illustrates her administrative background and the responsibility entrusted to her.

The initial layout of her CV is very common. However, including all this information at the beginning of her CV draws attention to her personal circumstances rather than to her skills and experience.

Clare also used initials, *eg* SMP and SSP, when describing her payroll duties. Although most readers would be expected to understand what these stood for, she may want to consider writing these out in full in future.

We commented on Clare's profile in the previous chapter, so in summary, Clare has an effective CV which compensates well for her lack of recent paid employment. Moving her personal details towards the end of the CV could help this to become even more effective.

Joanne Taylor's CV

Joanne Taylor BA

15 Cherrybush Avenue   Date of Birth: 7 March 1984
Killingdon   Full Clean Driving Licence
Stoke on Trent   Status: Single
ST12 0TL

PROFILE
A commercially aware graduate with experience in retail.
Communicates well at all levels and enjoys motivating and
organising others. Works well under pressure and to tight
deadlines. Takes great pride in seeing a task through from start to
finish.

QUALIFICATIONS

2002 – 2006	Bradford University – BA Hons. degree in Applied Social Studies (incorporating social work qualification).
1994 – 2001	Longton High School: 3 'A' Levels: Sociology (B), Psychology (B), General Studies (C). 8 GCSEs including English (A) and Maths (C).

WORK EXPERIENCE

2006	Acting Probation Officer as part of a work placement, managing a case load of juvenile clients. Involved with client visits both at home and in Youth Custody Centre. Dealt with a wide range of people, including Magistrates, Solicitors, Police and School Teachers.

2005	Wheatfields Hospice, Leeds. • Nursed terminally ill cancer patients whilst on a work placement.
2001 – 2002	'Rannigans' (whilst in 6th form) • Worked as a sales assistant within a large retail outlet employing 40 staff. • Involved in serving and answering customer queries. • Handling cash and carried out stock taking and merchandising.
1999 – 2001	Bennets Sports Ltd – Sales Assistant • Worked on Saturdays and during summer holidays as a sales assistant in a busy sports shop. Responsible for cashing up and managing the store in the manager's absence.

INTERESTS

Enjoy foreign travel which I have been able to do during University vacations. Keen on most sports, particularly swimming and rowing.

ADDITIONAL INFORMATION

Active member of the Student Union and the Debating Society. Elected Finance Secretary of University Rowing Club.

Comments

Joanne's CV is different from the others examined so far. This is no surprise, as her background and future intentions are also different. Joanne aims to gain a position within an organisation as a graduate management trainee and therefore attention is drawn to her academic achievements.

She includes personal details at the beginning of her CV, but in this case that is not likely to be detrimental. The mention of a clean driving licence is beneficial, as not all graduates would possess one and this is another point in her favour.

Her profile emphasises her commercial awareness, as she seeks to deal with the issue of having gained a Social Work oriented degree as opposed to a business one. The personal attributes mentioned in her profile, *eg* 'motivating', 'organising', 'working to tight deadlines', would all be of benefit in the business world. (As we will see in Chapter 7, the key will be to back up all these statements with concrete examples.)

Joanne outlines the course title of her degree, but fails to mention what classification she received and what subjects she studied as part of her course.

Joanne deals well with her work experience, which is always relevant to the reader. The ability to demonstrate not just academic qualifications, but some form of practical work experience, no matter how basic, will always be an advantage. Joanne is particularly fortunate that her degree included work placements that provided her with such stimulating experience. Her work as a sales assistant is also relevant and no matter what work you have done, even if only on a temporary basis, it is always worth promoting.

In an additional information section Joanne highlights her student activities. This is a good idea, although Joanne could have developed further the skills she acquired through her involvement in the Student Union and as Finance Secretary for the Rowing Club.

Joanne has produced a good CV which can be developed even further.

Brian Lynch's CV

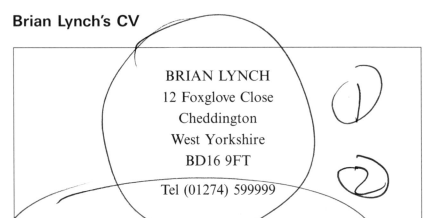

BRIAN LYNCH
12 Foxglove Close
Cheddington
West Yorkshire
BD16 9FT

Tel (01274) 599999

An excellent man manager with 9 years' supervisory experience. Communicates well at all levels and has developed a wide range of practical skills. Intelligent, with the ability to solve problems using initiative and a creative approach.

Key Skills/Experience gained whilst being responsible for the supervision of staff and multimillion pound equipment within a major industrial complex.

- Manage and supervise 50 staff on a regular basis and up to 200 on occasions.
- Liaising and consulting with senior management on matters relating to productivity and safe practices.
- Motivating and inspiring colleagues to achieve optimum productivity whilst working to strict deadlines.
- Implementing health and safety regulations.
- Originating the deployment of staff over a 3 shift system and being accountable for both productivity and work standards.

- Checking the performance and suitability of safety equipment.

Career History

(1981 – 2006) British Coal/UK Coal plc

(1997 – 2006) Supervisor (Deputy)

(1981 – 1995) Production and Haulage Work

Training

- Completed Supervisors course which included Management, Communication and Team Building skills. Also incorporated health and safety and work related legislation.
- On the job training in the operation and maintenance of a wide range of heavy industrial equipment.

Personal Details

Status: Divorced

Date of Birth: 8th September 1965

Clean driving licence and a non smoker

Interests

Fishing, golf and DIY

Comments

Brian's aim was to sell his management skills and not to 'litter' his CV with constant references to mining. We saw in Chapter 3 how successful he had been in relation to outlining his key skills and experience. Brian's profile targets his intention to stay in a management role, but is general enough to apply to any particular industry.

Brian has worked for British Coal for 25 years, but much of this experience is now irrelevant and is omitted from his CV. His job title at British Coal was Deputy, which will mean very little to anyone outside the industry. He therefore refers to himself as a 'Supervisor'.

Brian left school without taking any exams and has decided not to include a section on education in his CV as it will not enhance his application.

Brian has successfully compiled a CV that emphasises his management skills, which, although acquired in mining, are easily transferable to other industries.

ACTION AND REFLECTION

Action points

1 It may appropriate to have more than one version of your CV.
2 Different styles of CV are useful to have, depending on your circumstances and objectives.
3 Your CV must look good and be easy to read.
4 We can tailor our CV to a particular job in order to draw attention to relevant skills and experience.
5 Jargon should only be used when we know the reader will understand it.
6 There is no perfect way to write a CV, only 'an appropriate way'.

Points to consider

♦ How honest are we being when we deliberately tailor our CV?
♦ Where would you place your personal details on a CV?
♦ Why has the style of CVs changed so much in recent years?

5

Getting the Introductions Right

PLANNING A GREAT COVERING LETTER

You are now well on the way to having a CV that will arouse interest in the reader and win you interviews. So why do we need a covering letter to go along with it?

- Your letter can further tailor your application by expanding on certain points from your CV.

- A professionally presented letter adds to the overall impact of your CV.

- As you can pay to have your CV done by an agency, some companies place greater emphasis on your letter, as it is more likely to be all your own work.

- Taking the trouble to write a letter further highlights your interest in the position.

When do I use a covering letter?
Use a covering letter whenever you are contacting an organisation or person with your CV. The only exception to this is when you are asked specifically not to do so, or when an agency is submitting a CV on your behalf.

Will all organisations read my covering letter?
No. Some people will only be interested in reading your CV. However, as we don't know who these people are before we apply, it is always better to write a covering letter.

How long should my letter be?

Usually no more than one side of A4. However, some of the first page will be taken up with their address and yours. So you may go on to a second page. As a guide, your actual letter (excluding addresses) should be no more than one page.

HANDWRITING OR WORD-PROCESSED?

Opinion varies as to which is best to do. Ultimately, it is a personal choice. Let's examine some of the advantages of both.

Advantages of handwriting

◆ If your writing is neat, it can help your letter stand out from the crowd.

◆ The reader may be impressed at the trouble you have gone to in writing a letter.

◆ The letter gives your application a more personal touch.

Advantages of word processing

◆ Your letter will appear more business-like and professional.

◆ You are able to include more information in less space than with a hand-written letter.

◆ Your letter will be easier to read.

You may of course have no choice, if you do not have access to a computer. If this is the case, you have three choices:

1 Pay to have your letter word-processed.
2 Get to know someone who has access to a computer.
3 Buy yourself a good pen!

PUTTING A POSITIVE LETTER TOGETHER

Too many good CVs can be hindered by a poor covering letter. So what constitutes an ineffective covering letter?

◆ Poor layout.
◆ Cheap quality paper.
◆ Typing or spelling mistakes.
◆ Disorganised style.
◆ Failure to 'sell yourself' to the reader.

An example of a poorly written covering letter is as follows:

---

33 Western Road
Wokingham
Surrey

Dear Sir or Madam,

I am writing to apply for the position of finance officer. I enclose my CV for your peruesal and would be available for interview at your convenience.

Hope to hear from you shorty

Yours sincerely

Kevin Proctor (Mr)

It is not uncommon for people to send such a letter with a CV. Let's examine it in more detail.

Layout
The letter is poorly laid out. The address is incomplete with no post code or telephone number. The letter is not dated and the recipient's address is not included.

Spelling
Presumably a finance officer would have to pay close attention to detail. The writer fails to do so in this case, spelling the word 'perusal' as 'peruesal'. Missing the 'l' out of 'shortly', although amusing, could also be seen as offensive!

Style
The letter is addressed to 'Dear Sir or Madam'. It would seem no initiative has been taken to find out the person's name. The letter is also finished incorrectly by using the phrase 'Yours sincerely' rather than 'Yours faithfully'. Also the use of phrases such as 'for your perusal' and 'at your convenience' are rather trite standard phrases and say very little.

Failure to sell yourself
A covering letter provides an ideal opportunity for the writer to sell themselves. This letter fails completely to attract the reader's attention or enhance or elaborate on the enclosed CV.

An effective covering letter
That was an example of an ineffective letter. So what should a good letter look like? The layout should appear as in Figure 11.

Fig. 11. Example layout of a covering letter.

A positive covering letter should:

- be written or typed on good quality paper
- be well laid out and easy to follow
- arouse interest as an introduction to your CV
- be free from typing or spelling mistakes
- sell you by highlighting key points relevant to the reader's requirements
- create a positive impact.

Many people will be able to lay out the letter in the correct way and even present it neatly. However, the main stumbling block comes when writing the contents of the letter. What should be included in this section? The following is a guide which can be adapted accordingly.

Reason for writing

You may be responding to a specific advert or enquiring about future vacancies. Alternatively, you may wish to offer your services as a self employed person. Whatever the case, set out your stall from the start.

Refer to your CV and emphasise relevant points

Highlight and elaborate on points in your CV that directly relate to the advert. Do not simply re-hash your CV. However, do not be afraid to repeat certain statements. If your letter is not related to a specific position, then this section will be more general.

Personality

Although this is not easy to convey on paper, weave into your letter phrases that express your personality. You may include similar statements to those in your profile. Relate these aspects of your personality to the role in question.

Polite and positive ending

Do not end your letter in an abrupt fashion. Why are you sending this letter with your CV? In order to gain an interview or meeting. Therefore, end your letter on a positive and polite note. For example:

'I believe I possess the necessary skills and experience you require and look forward to the opportunity of discussing the position in more detail.'

NOT

'I hope to hear from you shortly.'

A good covering letter will not compensate for a poor CV. It will, however, add to the overall impression of your application. The letter is likely to be read before your CV. How the reader views your letter will influence his/her reading of your CV. Although we cannot be sure how much attention will be given to our letter, our aim must be to present a professional and positive letter that makes the reader think: 'Very impressive. Their CV should make interesting reading.'

APPLYING OVER THE INTERNET

More and more organisations, particularly job agencies, are asking individuals to e-mail their CVs. The advantage to you is primarily:

◆ Your CV gets to the recruiter more quickly.
◆ You save on postage and paper.

However, beware of the following when sending your CV as an attachment:

♦ The receiver may be concerned that an attachment may contain viruses.

♦ The receiver may not possess the appropriate software to open your attachment. Technology may alter the style, format and layout of your CV.

If the organisation you are applying to does not accept attachments, or is unable to open them, then I suggest you cut and paste your text file CV into the bottom of the e-mail itself.

Remember, applying over the Internet should not alter the style of your CV. The methodology you use to communicate may change, but what you communicate doesn't need to.

ANALYSING A JOB ADVERT

Much of the content of our letter will be determined by what is in the advert. Unfortunately, not all adverts are very helpful to the reader. They can:

♦ be vague and lacking in detail concerning the position
♦ omit key requirements of the job
♦ misinform or mislead
♦ make extravagant claims regarding earnings
♦ give little or no detail about the organisation.

Sometimes it may be possible to telephone the organisation for more information. When this is not possible, we must simply do the best we can with the information we have. However, a poor advert may be sending you signals about the organisation and their professionalism.

LOOKING AT SOME EXAMPLES

Example 1

Production Supervisor Required
for
The Manning Metal Group

We are a large and growing organisation with a £20m per annum turnover. We operate on a global level, producing and distributing metal products throughout the world.

Due to our expansion we now require a Production Supervisor who is able to deliver results in a manufacturing environment. Applications are welcome from people able to demonstrate a successful track record to date in manufacturing. A hands on approach, excellent management and problem solving skills are also necessary. Qualifications are desirable but not essential.

Please write with CV to:

The Managing Director
The Manning Metal Group
Hounslow Road
Bury
Manchester
M15 2FJ

Fig. 12. A sample job advertisement.

This advert gives the reader a fair degree of information. The question is, when responding to such an advert, where do you begin?

Firstly, underline or highlight the key words in the advert, stating what the company requires from the applicant. You may find it helpful to write it down as follows:

	They require	**I've got**
1	_____	_____
2	_____	_____
3	_____	_____
4	_____	_____
5	_____	_____
6	_____	_____

Having done this, you may decide you do not have the experience or skills required. If you do have appropriate skills or experience, you are in a position to outline in your letter how these match their requirements. You may also want to tailor your CV accordingly.

The key requirement needed by someone applying for this job would be:

1   Ability to deliver results in a manufacturing environment.
2   Successful track record in manufacturing.
3   Hands on approach.
4   Excellent man management skills.
5   Excellent problem solving skills.
6   Qualifications desirable but not essential.

We also know from the advert:

◆   the name and annual spend of the company
◆   what the company does and where its markets are.

These factors will influence our reply. However, it is important that **we address the specific requirements of the applicant**.

Our letter must therefore demonstrate:

- a successful track record in manufacturing with an emphasis on achieving results
- a hands on approach
- excellent man management and problem solving skills.

Although the company requires a production supervisor, this is only the title **they** give to the position. It may well be that the successful applicant is able to demonstrate all the necessary skills and experience but had a different job title. The key in analysing an advert is to **pay attention to the skills and experience required for the job, not just to the job title**.

The advert also states that qualifications are desirable but not essential. In my experience, if you do not possess all the essential requirements, you are unlikely to be successful in your application. However, words used such as 'ideally', 'preferably' and 'desirable' indicate that if you do not possess these requirements, it is still worth applying.

Example 2

Cashiers needed

Are you friendly, reliable and self motivated? Do you enjoy dealing with the public and have a flexible approach to work? Are you able to work under pressure using your own initiative?

If so, we require full time and part time cashiers to work within our busy 24 hour petrol station. You will be required to work shifts, including some weekends. Telephone and own transport are essential. Full training will be given.

Please apply in writing, enclosing CV, to
Mrs S Johnson, Byron Garages, Luton Rd., Luton.

Fig. 13. A sample job advertisement.

Applying the same method of analysis, the requirements would be:

1   Friendly.
2   Reliable.
3   Self motivated.
4   Enjoy dealing with the public.
5   Flexible approach to work.
6   Able to work under pressure.
7   Use own initiative.

Our letter and CV must therefore demonstrate these qualities. This is not easy to do, as requirements such as 'friendly' are difficult to express on paper and is a quality open to opinion rather than fact. However, if we are to have a chance of gaining an interview, we must demonstrate in writing our ability to do this job.

Analysing the advert will also help prepare us for our interview. The advert states what kind of person the organisation is looking for, so when it comes to the interview, it will be up to us to tailor our answers accordingly.

CASE STUDIES

Clare Griffiths demonstrates initiative

Clare saw the following advert in her local paper.

Sales Advisers Required   **Salary Neg.**
Bebbingtons Estate Agents require Sales Advisers to join its successful team working in our branches throughout Cheshire.

Successful applicants will be mature, with an outgoing personality and must enjoy dealing with a wide range of people. Enthusiasm and initiative are more desirable than academic qualifications, as is previous sales experience. You will be required to work flexible hours including some weekend work and must have a clean driving licence.

Please apply in writing enclosing CV to J. Marston, Area Manager, Bebbington Estate Agents, Nantwich, Cheshire, CW12 3PF.

Clare's first task is to analyse the advert. She identifies the key requirements as follows:

They require	I've got
Mature	Yes
Outgoing personality	Yes
Deal with a wide range of people	From crèche workers to MPs
Enthusiasm	Yes, involvement with PTA
Initiative	Approaching local MP
Flexible hours	No problem
Clean driving licence	Yes
Desirable	Do not have any
Sales experience	experience.

Clare realises she has no previous sales experience; however, as this requirement is only desirable, she is still prepared to apply. She believes she meets all other requirements. Clare also demonstrates her initiative by contacting the Estate Agents to ascertain whether J Marston is a man or a woman. She is therefore able to address Mrs Marston accordingly.

Mrs J Marston	14 Bronwich Close
Area Manager	Stockton Heath
Bebbington Estate Agents	Warrington
Nantwich	Cheshire
Cheshire	WA4 2FL
CW12 3PF	Tel 01925 333335

25th April 20XX

Dear Mrs Marston

Re: Sales Advisers Position

I was very interested to read of your requirements for Sales Advisers and enclose my CV in connection with this.

As you will see from my CV, my career began in banking, where I dealt with the public on a daily basis. Whilst managing a busy household and raising 2 children, I have continued to deal with a wide range of people including my MP. Due to the lack of child care facilities in the area, I demonstrated my initiative by taking action, hence my contact with the local Member of Parliament.

I consider myself outgoing, with plenty of enthusiasm, which is necessary, particularly in relation to raising funds for the school PTA.

Flexible hours present no problems, as provision has already been made for my children. I have held a clean driving licence for 17 years and have a thorough knowledge of Cheshire.

I am currently training on a word processor course, which would, I am sure, be a useful skill within a busy office environment. Obviously, it is not easy to fully convey my interpersonal skills on paper, therefore I look forward to meeting you to discuss the position in more detail.

Yours sincerely

(Mrs Clare Griffiths)

Comments

This is an excellent example of a covering letter.

♦ The layout is correct and she has demonstrated initiative (a requirement for the position) by finding out the title of J Marston.

♦ The opening 'I was very interested...' conveys enthusiasm – again, a requirement for the job.

♦ The letter is well structured and addresses all the key requirements apart from her maturity. This could be ascertained from her age, which is stated in her CV.

♦ Clare briefly backs up her skills with examples, *eg* working in a bank, contact with local MP and work for the school PTA.

- Any possible concern the reader might have about her availability to work flexible hours is also dealt with, again briefly.

- Clare does not draw attention to her lack of sales experience; where she states at the end 'I look forward to meeting you' is a positive note to finish on and one that would be expected from a person working in sales.

Joanne Taylor's letter could be better

Joanne saw the following vacancies advertised in a national newspaper.

Graduate Trainees Required – Personnel Function

Hemmings the Retailers requires graduates of outstanding calibre to train in all aspects of Personnel Management. As the company has a number of sites nationally, successful applicants must be prepared to be mobile for the first 2 years.

Hemmings offers first class training and actively encourages successful applicants to study for professional qualifications. The company has an active policy of developing its staff and therefore rapid career advancement is possible. A competitive salary along with usual benefits is on offer.

CVs are welcome from graduates able to demonstrate excellent communication and interpersonal skills, who thrive on the challenges of a constantly changing environment. Please also state what appeals to you about a career in personnel and why you believe you can contribute to our success.

Write enclosing your CV to Gary Cole, Graduate Recruitment Officer, Hemmings Ltd., Victoria House, Basford, Nottingham NG7 4PD.

Joanne analyses the advertisement and drafts the following reply.

Mr Gary Cole   15 Cherrybush Ave
Graduate Recruitment Officer   Killingdon
Hemmings Ltd   Stoke on Trent
Victoria House   ST12 0TL
Basford
Nottingham
NG7 4PD

2nd May 20XX

Dear Gary

<u>Re: Graduate Trainees – Personnel Function</u>

Please find enclosed my CV in connection with the above.

As my CV indicates, I have already gained experience in the retail industry and am keen to continue this within the Personnel function.

Having discussed with several people the role of personnel within an organisation, I am excited at the prospect of being involved in such an area. The recent merger of the Institute of Personnel Management with the ITD is, I believe, a positive step and indicates the significant role the Human Resource function has to play in business. I see personnel related in broad terms to the 'management of people within an organisation' and as people are an organisation's biggest asset, I see this as the kind of challenging position I require.

My excellent communication skills were developed during my time at university, where I was used to addressing large audiences through my involvement with the Student Union and also on a one to one basis in other capacities.

The retail industry is going through many changes at present, with the onset of foreign competition and 'home shopping'. These are exciting and challenging times and I believe I possess the necessary drive, commitment and dedication to help ensure that Hemmings Ltd continues to be successful.

I look forward to the opportunity of discussing the position in more detail.

Yours sincerely

Joanne Taylor

Comments

This is an example of a good letter, although there are two areas of concern:

◆ Joanne's letter is addressed to Gary rather than Mr Cole. There is no definite right or wrong answer to how he should have been addressed. However, using his first name may be seen as being over familiar. It is better to err on the side of caution in most cases and therefore 'Mr Cole' would be more appropriate.

♦ The advert specified that mobility was required. Joanne has failed to address this in her letter. The reader may assume she is mobile because she has applied; however, her letter would have been improved if she had addressed all the issues in the advert.

The good points of the letter are:

♦ Joanne addresses the issue of why she wants to work in personnel and develops this by showing a knowledge of background related issues.

♦ Evidence of her 'excellent communication skills' is backed up with an example from her involvement with the Student Union.

♦ Her ending is positive and also shows an understanding of the challenges the retail industry is facing. The impression she creates is that this is not 'any old job', but one she is interested in and has researched.

ACTION AND REFLECTION

Action points

1 A well written covering letter can greatly enhance your job application.
2 The main purpose of the letter is to motivate the recipient to read your CV.
3 Your letter can help tailor and personalise your application by emphasising relevant points.
4 Like your CV, your letter may differ in length and style, depending on your objectives and the situation.

5 Always analyse an advert and identify requirements before writing your letter.

6 Ensure your letter is correctly laid out and is well presented.

7 Purchase a pad of quality paper.

Points to consider

◆ How important have your considered covering letters to be in the past?

◆ How up to date are you on the style of letters today and how they are laid out?

◆ What difficulties are faced by people drafting job advertisements?

Using Your CV to Open Doors

Now you have a brilliantly effective CV and you know how to write a covering letter that will stimulate the interest of the reader. But there is another important piece of the jigsaw to consider.

TAPPING INTO THE UNADVERTISED JOB MARKET

Many people limit themselves to using their CV only in response to advertised vacancies, completely ignoring the hidden job market. I say hidden, because of the startling statistic that:

75% of jobs are never advertised.

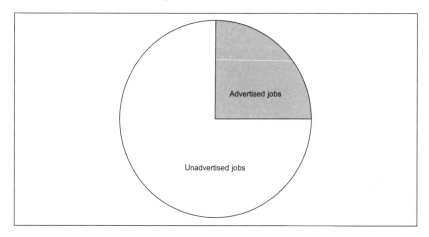

Fig. 14. Proportion of unadvertised jobs.

Most people seeking employment concentrate their efforts on only 25% of the pie! (The exact figures are difficult to come by, but it is commonly accepted that around three quarters of jobs available are not advertised.)

Why is this?

Jobs are not advertised because:

◆ It is a time consuming business.

◆ Jobs can be filled internally.

◆ They may have a file full of CVs already.

◆ The cost involved is too high.

◆ Selection procedures are not reliable. They may not end up with the right person anyway.

◆ Companies are swamped with applicants.

◆ They may not want competitors to know they are recruiting.

So the main advantage to a company not advertising a position is that they **save time and money**.

Organisations which adhere to strict equal opportunities guidelines will, in most cases, advertise vacancies. These tend to be the larger institutions which have the resources and expertise to handle recruitment.

What to consider when you make a speculative approach

Advantages

You are at the front of the queue.

The queue may not be very long.

You have demonstrated initiative.

Disadvantages

You have to contact a lot of companies to increase your chances of success.

You must get used to rejection.

You must get used to hearing nothing.

There is one factor which I believe will contribute to our success: **luck**. In other words:

Making contact with the right company at the right time.

However, there is a saying which I have found to be true:

'The more I do, the luckier I become.'

Making speculative approaches, as we are about to see, can be time consuming. Yet as we do more, we increase our chances of success.

HOW TO SPECULATE

There are a variety of ways to tap into the unadvertised jobs market. These approaches are equally applicable if you are self employed or currently studying and looking to secure a placement.

Newspapers

Both local and national papers can be a rich source of information. They offer:

♦ articles about companies expanding, or which have won new orders

♦ advance news of a new company moving into the area

♦ information about new business park developments

♦ recruitment advertisements including contact names and addresses of companies recruiting.

It is not uncommon to see such headlines as 'Stoke Company Set To Expand', 'Smith Ltd To Open New Factory In Bolton' or '200 Jobs To Be Created In New Business Park'.

So you will benefit from reading the papers, especially the business section, every day, and not just when you expect jobs to be advertised.

The Internet

Finding out about organisations has never been so easy since the growth of the Internet. The challenge is wading through the amount of information available. One excellent site to visit is *www.uk businesspark.co.uk* which has a section called 'Opportunities for Employment'. This provides information on employers who are expanding and recruiting large numbers of staff. You might be able to contact the organisation before these 'intended' jobs have been advertised. You could also visit *www.europages.com* which lists companies by industry type (*eg* IT) and you can narrow your search by focusing on particular locations. Alternatively, if you are interested in particular companies you can phone and ask for their website address.

The library

Many people I speak to stopped visiting the library about the same time they stopped believing in Father Christmas! Yet the library can provide you with so much information. Make it part of your action plan to visit one as soon as possible. Not only can you read the newspapers for free, but also other materials that can provide you with a wealth of information. These include:

Business directories

A number of directories can be found in a good reference library, such *Kompass* or *Kellys*. The information they contain about companies includes:

- name, address and telephone number
- financial turnover
- number of employees
- product range or services offered
- names of owners or directors.

This information is useful because it answers two important questions:

1   Is this the kind of company (*ie* size, type of business) that I want to work for?

2   Who is the person I should write to?

People fall into the trap of ignoring the second question. As we saw in Chapter 2, one of the reasons our CV may fail is because it was not read by the right person. This happens because, for example, if we write to a job title such as the personnel manager:

- such a position may not even exist

- even if it does, as it is not specifically addressed to a named person, it is more likely to be read by a junior member of staff and the decision maker may never see it.

The chances of our CV being read are increased if it is addressed to a named person. Consider this point. We all receive junk mail through our letter box. What are we most likely to read, items addressed to 'The Occupier' or those addressed to us personally?

As these directories can sometimes be out of date, it is always useful to phone first of all, either to check the name of the person or, if you have been unable to find a contact name, simply to ask for one. Most companies will usually divulge this information. If they don't, you may find help from another source...

USING YOUR CONTACTS

It's not what you know, it's who you know

From my experience, this seems to be increasingly the case. Some people do feel uncomfortable approaching their contacts when looking for work or new business. This is usually because:

- Some people prefer to be judged solely on their own merits and do not want to gain an unfair advantage over others.

- People do not want to appear 'pushy' by approaching contacts and possibly jeopardising their relationship.

However, it is worth remembering that:

- Companies prefer to interview and recruit people who have been recommended to them.

- The majority of people may be flattered that you have approached them and will probably be only too willing to help.

A lot will depend on your attitude and approach.

How to make the approach

This will depend on the relationship you have with the person. It is important to remember the following:

> **You are not asking for a job, but for advice
> and information that may lead to one.**

As long as people are clear about what you are asking for, there should not be a problem.

What advice or information could they give you?

♦ The name of a person in the organisation to contact about vacancies.

♦ They could collect an application form for you to complete.

♦ They could inform you of any vacancies they may be aware of.

♦ They could suggest places for you to apply to.

♦ They could give advice concerning your CV. (Asking people for comments about your CV is a subtle way of informing them of all the skills and experience you have!)

♦ They may not be able to help you themselves, but may be able to put you in contact with someone who can.

Who to contact

Some people say, 'but I don't really know anyone.' Really? Let's look at some potential contacts (Figure 15).

Within each category, there may be many people you can list. It is often surprising how many people we come into contact with on a

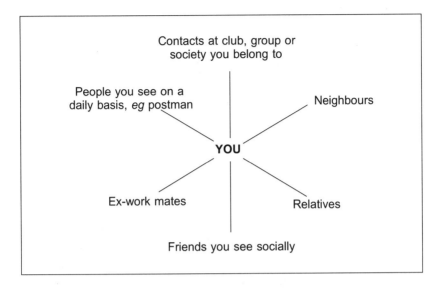

Fig. 15. Your potential contacts.

regular basis. Some of these people we will hardly know, but they could all be a potential source of help.

Take some time now to think about the people you have contact with, or could approach for help. Then do the following:

1   Review your activities over the last two weeks and write down who you have come into contact with (*eg* postman, neighbours, shop assistants, relatives, friends, work colleagues, students, mobile hairdressers *etc...*).

2   Look through your address book and diary and make a note of all your contacts.

3   Now list those people likely to be of some assistance to you. You should be able to list at least 20 names.

Name	Address + telephone number	Action to be taken

Our contacts can be a tremendous source of help. Having developed a winning CV, we should make sure as many people as possible see it.

MAKING YOURSELF KNOWN – HOW AGENCIES CAN HELP

Increasingly, companies are using agencies to recruit through. There are two types of agencies:

Jobs agencies or employment agencies

These agencies provide staff for organisations, usually on a temporary short-term basis. The agency will charge the company a fee and the individual is paid by the agency. In uncertain economic times, many organisations are 'employing' staff in this way. The main advantages to employers are:

♦ They can give notice at any time, without going through any lengthy procedures.

♦ They can recruit and lay off staff in keeping with the work flow, *eg* seasonal work.

♦ There is less 'risk' with temporary staff.

♦ Although the agency has to be paid, the company does not have to worry about pension provisions, national insurance contributions or holiday pay.

♦ The companies does not have to advertise and handle the recruitment process.

This does have implications for you.

Advantages of working for agencies

◆ It can provide valuable work experience.

◆ Because of the variety of work available, it demonstrates your flexibility and willingness to work.

◆ It can bring a routine to your day and an opportunity to meet people.

◆ It may provide you with the opportunity to learn new skills.

◆ The company you work for may offer you full time employment.

Disadvantages of working for agencies

◆ The pay is usually lower than for permanent staff.

◆ You have few legal rights.

◆ With few exceptions, if you don't work, you receive no holiday or sick pay.

◆ There is a lack of security. It can be difficult to plan ahead.

The choice as to whether you work for an agency is up to you. You must weigh up the pros and cons. However, it is yet another approach in which your CV can play a vital role. An agency needs to know what you have done and the skills that you possess in order to match you with a suitable vacancy.

To contact a job agency, look in *Yellow Pages* under 'Employment Agencies and Consultants'.

Recruitment consultancies

Although they recruit on behalf of a company, that is all they do. Once someone has been successfully placed, they usually have nothing else to do with the agency.

So why do companies use them?

◆ For business reasons. They may not want to publicise to a competitor the fact that they have a vacancy.

◆ They may lack expertise in recruitment matters.

◆ Using agencies saves them the time spent handling the recruitment process.

Recruitment consultants will often advertise a position on behalf of their client. However, they have a database of potential candidates, some of whom may be put forward for the position without it being advertised. Therefore, it is worth contacting recruitment consultancies with your CV. If you wish to contact a recruitment consultant, look at the *Executive Grapevine*, which lists names and addresses of recruitment consultants and agencies. Some consultancies specialise in particular sectors and this information is provided in the book.

Whichever type of agency you come across, your CV will be your main calling card. By contacting an agency with your CV you increase your chances of achieving success. This is the case whether you want:

◆ full-time permanent work
◆ temporary work
◆ part-time work
◆ self employment.

Self employed people can often find temporary assignments through an agency.

PUTTING YOUR SPECULATING INTO ACTION

Having explored a number of ways of tapping into the unadvertised jobs market, the next question is what approach to take. You have four options:

1   Ring the company/person/agency and arrange a meeting.

2   Visit the company/person/agency on spec.

3   Write to the company/person/agency and follow up with a phone call to arrange a meeting.

4   Register your details on-line with any of the job agency Internet sites. Job sites such as Monster Board, Top Jobs on the Net and Stepstone all advertise jobs. By registering your details with them you are also reaching potential employers. Some sites allow employers to search their sites for suitable candidates. By registering, sites can also automatically e-mail you details of any new jobs which fall within your particular requirements.

Whichever approach you take your CV will ultimately be the key to open the door.

If you phone
The person may say 'well send me your CV'.

If you visit
The person may say 'let me see your CV' or 'leave your CV with me'.

If you write
This is the approach most people feel comfortable with. When we write, we would enclose our CV.

In Chapter 5 we looked at the importance of covering letters. Our approach in writing on a speculative basis will be different in some ways, as we are not responding to a particular advert. It will also vary depending on who we are writing to. Bearing in mind the points raised in Chapter 5, also consider the following.

When writing to a company

- Write to a named person and use their correct job title.

- Outline your reasons for writing and enclose a CV.

- Sell your skills and experience rather than enquire about a specific position.

- Suggest a meeting not an interview.

- Commit yourself to taking follow up action by suggesting you will follow up with a phone call.

When writing to a contact

- Be open about your reasons for writing.

- Enclose your CV and invite opinions on it.

- Ask for help and advice in your job search, as opposed to asking for a job.

- Suggest a meeting or phone call.

- Keep the letter low key and friendly.

When writing to an agency

- State your reasons for writing.

- Enclose a CV that highlights your broad range of skills (a functional CV may be your best option).

- Outline where you are prepared to work.

- Indicate the kind of company you would envisage working for, *eg* size, type of business etc.

- Give a salary range.

- Tell them you will ring to follow this letter up.

When contacting an agency we can afford to be more 'up front' and direct about our position and objectives. A more 'softly softly' approach is usually best when approaching a company or personal contact.

Remember, as our personal requirements and objectives differ, so too will our approach. I have outlined some guidelines for you to follow, but each approach will vary according to your own individual situation.

Beware of e-mailing your CV speculatively

Technology may in some cases have decreased the amount of 'hard copy' (*ie* paper format) we receive. But it has also increased the amount of information we receive. It is not uncommon for managers to receive 50 e-mails a day. Pressing the delete button takes even less time than finding a bin! Therefore, in your speculation, stick to the more traditional approaches.

**It's easier to press a delete button
than it is to say 'no' to a person.**

CASE STUDIES

Colin Burrows approaches a contact

Colin Burrows has decided to start using his network. An old friend of his, John Banner, is marketing director for a biscuit manufacturer. Colin has not spoken to John for over a year, but still considers him a good friend who would be happy to help if he can.

---

22 Leeming Way
Vale Park
Warrington
Cheshire
WA9 2PF

19th October 20XX

Dear John

It has been some time since we last spoke and I thought now was an appropriate moment to contact you.

As you may be aware, my company was recently taken over and this has led to the inevitable 'restructuring process'. To put it bluntly, people are being made redundant and I have fallen into that category.

Knowing of your experience in the business world, I would be grateful if we could meet up and I could 'pick your brains'. I would be particularly grateful for your comments on my CV which I enclose with this letter.

Hope you, Linda and the kids are well. Mine as usual are driving me up the wall.

I'll give you a call sometime in the next week, thanks for your time

Kind regards

Colin

Comments

◆ The letter is informally laid out, keeping the personal touch, and could equally well have been hand-written if Colin had felt more comfortable with that.

◆ Colin gets quickly to the point of his letter, rather than slipping it in at the end.

◆ His situation is mentioned briefly without going into too much detail.

◆ The emphasis is on 'picking your brains' rather than on asking for a job.

◆ Colin encloses his CV which gives John an opportunity to study it rather than looking at it cold when they meet.

◆ The ending is friendly and personal.

◆ Colin will take the initiative to call 'sometime' rather than putting pressure on John to make the first move.

Overall impression
Colin's letter is brief, friendly and to the point. His informal

approach and use of language is unlikely to make John feel threatened, but neither is he left with any doubt about Colin's predicament.

Brian Lynch writes to an agency

Brian has decided to start contacting agencies and has identified Chase Recruitment in Halifax as one that specialises in senior and middle management positions.

Philip Daniels   12 Foxglove Close
Chase Recruitment   Cheddington
Lancaster House   West Yorkshire
Meadow Way   BD16 9FT
Halifax   24th October 20XX
HX2 TY

Dear Mr Daniels

I enclose my CV for your attention. As you will see, I have nearly 10 years' management experience gained within a multi-million pound operation.

The contraction of the mining industry has presented me with an ideal opportunity to develop my career further and to utilise my skills and experience to date. Ideally I would like to remain in manufacturing and would consider a position anywhere in the UK.

Realistically, I am looking for a salary in the region of £25–£30k, although to a certain extent this depends on the location.

I will telephone you next Tuesday to arrange a meeting and to discuss further the opportunities that exist with your clients.

Yours sincerely

Brian Lynch

Comments

◆ Brian's letter is presented as a business letter and is formally set out.

◆ The opening paragraph is brief and to the point.

◆ Agencies are bombarded with CVs, they do not want to wade through a lengthy covering letter.

◆ Brian is honest about his situation, '... the contraction of the mining industry', and also positive: 'has presented me with an ideal opportunity to develop my career further'.

◆ He steers away from constant references to mining and instead uses terms such as '...a multi-million pound operation', and 'I would like to remain in manufacturing'.

◆ He clearly states his salary expectations and willingness to be mobile. However, he indicates flexibility as well '... although to a certain extent this depends on location'.

◆ He is specific on when he will call. Agencies are dealing with hundreds of people, so he will take the initiative to make it happen.

Overall impression

An excellent example of a brief yet specific letter, which includes all the relevant details an agency would require at this stage. His language does not 'pigeon-hole' him in mining and also indicates that he is likely to be proactive and clear in his management style.

Joanne Taylor contacts a possible employer

Joanne Taylor has read recently that Krodan Ltd, a computer organisation is relocating to the Stoke-on-Trent area from Surrey. A possible expansion programme involving the likelihood of a further 50 jobs is expected.

Joanne has no contact name or address of the company's location in Surrey. However a quick telephone call firstly to directory enquiries and then to Krodan Ltd has given her all she needs. She has been advised to contact Kathy Kilner, head of Human Resources.

Kathy Kilner
Head of Human Resources
Krodan Ltd.
Fenton Business Estate
Ferningham
Surrey
S12 7BY

15 Cherrybush Ave.
Killingdon
Stoke-on-Trent
ST12 0TL

2nd November 20XX

Dear Ms Kilner

I was very interested to learn of your company's relocation to the Stoke-on-Trent area and the exciting opportunities that are to be created. As a social studies graduate from Keele University, I am keen to develop my career within Human Resources and am currently studying for my IPD qualification.

I possess a wide range of skills, which I outline in my enclosed CV, developed through my activities at university and during my work placement as a Probation Officer. These include my ability to deal with a wide range of people from all backgrounds, in a caring and professional manner. I would welcome the opportunity to discuss in more detail my experience to date and how I may contribute to the smooth and efficient running of your business.

I will telephone you next week, in order to discuss this matter further, at a time convenient to yourself.

Thank you for your kind attention.

Yours sincerely

Joanne Taylor

Comments

- By showing initiative, Joanne's enquiries have given her a name and job title to which to address this business letter. (She may also have tried to establish if Kathy Kilner was a Miss or a Mrs.)

- Her opening is positive, as she uses words like 'interested' and 'exciting'.

- She backs up her keenness to develop a career in human resources by her reference to studying for her IPD qualification. (In this instance IPD, short for Institute of Personnel and Development, can be used in an abbreviated form, as it is the main personnel qualification.)

- She refers briefly to her main skill, 'dealing with people', but fails to bring out the benefit of this.

- Her reference to 'smooth and effective running of your business' may be extremely pertinent bearing in mind the upheaval the company is likely to face in relocating.

- Her ending is positive and polite. Busy business people do not enjoy being rung out of the blue and reference to 'at a time convenient to yourself' is a courteous approach to take.

Overall impression

Joanne's letter is a good example of a targeted, speculative approach, and is both professional and polite. She could develop further the benefits to the organisation of her skills, but this lack would be unlikely to prevent her gaining an interview if there was a suitable position. A follow up call will also answer the question, 'when will they get back to me?'

ACTION AND SELF-ASSESSMENT

Action points

1 Having a good CV alone will not lead to success: we must know how to use it.

2 As the majority of jobs are never advertised, we must make speculative approaches to increase our chances of success.

3 Make use of newspapers, libraries, the Internet and friends in order to generate leads.

4 Always write to a person, not just a job title.

5 Writing, phoning, e-mailing and visiting are ways we can approach organisations.

6 Always suggest a meeting rather than an interview.

7 Do not pigeon-hole yourself into a particular job category.

Self-assessment

- How comfortable do you feel approaching friends or family for help in your job search? What kind of reaction do you expect from them?
- How do you feel about the amount of rejection you are likely to receive?
- What is worse for you, hearing 'no' or not hearing anything?

$$\boxed{7}$$

'And Your Chosen Subject Is . . .You' – The Interview

Your CV and letter have had the desired result – you have an interview. How do you prepare yourself for it?

PREPARING FOR YOUR INTERVIEW

Interviews can vary considerably in:

◆ style taken (informal/formal)
◆ length of time involved
◆ number of interviews in the selection process
◆ number of people conducting the interview
◆ the involvement of tests
◆ location (on site or off site)
◆ 'face to face' or 'over the phone'.

Having attended a number of interviews, I am aware that no two interviews are the same. However, in most cases, the role of the CV is central to the whole process. The level of importance attached to the CV by the interviewer will vary. In some cases, your CV may not have been seen, as the company asked you to complete an application form. Your CV, though, has acted as an aide-mémoire in filling in this form and the exercises completed in order to identify your skills and achievements have given you valuable personal insights, which will help your application.

With few exceptions, if you have applied with a CV, then this will provide the focal point for your interview.

If there is more than one interviewer, each will have a copy of your CV. It is not uncommon to see notes scribbled in the margins of your CV and certain points highlighted with a marker pen.

So if you approach an interview thinking: 'I wonder what they will ask me?' you already have a good idea.

THE TWO MAIN TYPES OF INTERVIEW

Let's examine the two main types of interview:

1   The telephone interview.
2   The face to face interview.

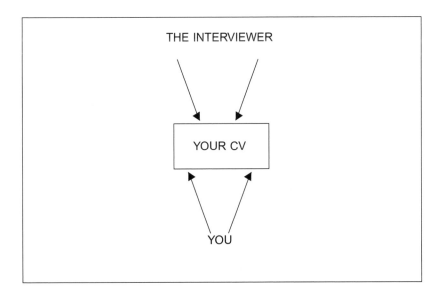

Fig. 16. The role of your CV at the interview.

Handling the telephone interview

Advertisements for jobs may end with the following:

> 'For more information and an informal discussion, please ring...'

> 'In the first instance telephone...'

> 'For an application form, please telephone the Personnel department on...'

Many people, without thinking, simply pick up the telephone and call. **Don't**. There may be a number of reasons why the company asked you to call.

◆ A list will be compiled of those people who did call. (This may be part of the criteria for the short listing process.)

◆ The company may disclose further information not included on the advert, which may aid your application.

◆ How well you communicate on the telephone may be vital for the position you are applying for. By inviting you to telephone, they are able to ascertain your ability.

◆ There is a high cost involved in sending out application forms. Asking you to telephone is a way in which to 'sift' the applicants.

◆ The vacancy may need to be filled quickly. A mini interview over the phone may then decide who is invited to a 'face to face'.

Be prepared before you phone

Of course, it may be none of the above. You may just be asked for your name and address and an application form will be sent to you.

You won't know for sure until you ring. So . . .

- ◆ Be prepared mentally. This may turn into a telephone interview.

- ◆ Re-read your CV before calling and have it ready to refer to whilst on the phone.

- ◆ Prepare a list of questions to highlight your interest in the company.

- ◆ Have a pen and paper ready to take notes.

- ◆ Choose a quiet place where you will be free from interruptions.

- ◆ Be positive and smile!

- ◆ Follow up your agreed action immediately. If asked to send your CV do so that day. Send it first class and to a named person

Preparing for your 'face to face'

Having secured an interview or meeting, half the battle is won before the interview begins. It is won due to one thing, **preparation**.

When we are asked to attend an interview, there are a number of issues to consider:

- ◆ Have I confirmed I can attend?
- ◆ Do I know how to get there?
- ◆ Do I know what kind of interview to expect?
- ◆ Have I practised the journey?
- ◆ What do I know about the company or the person I am meeting?
- ◆ Have I a list of questions to ask?
- ◆ Am I happy with my personal preparation?
- ◆ What certificates or testimonials will I be taking?

We can deal with all of the above and more, but still be very nervous and lacking in confidence. Why? Because we are wondering what questions will be asked. As you know, your CV is likely to be the focal point of your interview. So...

DISCOVER WHAT QUESTIONS THEY'RE BOUND TO ASK

There are only four things your interviewer wants to know:

1   Can you do the job?
2   Will you fit in?
3   Why do you want to work here?
4   How much will you work for?

But they have 101 ways of finding out the answers.

Can you do the job/work?

If you have gained an interview on the basis of your CV, the interviewer already thinks you can probably do the job. This impression will have been gained from reading about your work experience, training and qualifications. This can be developed by asking further questions during the interview, for example:

- What did you do in your last job?
- Describe a typical day.
- What would you do if...happened?

Or by

- a written test/exam
- performing a practical task.

Or by

♦ taking up references, with particular emphasis on your last employer's opinion of you.

Will you fit in?

Questions commonly asked include:

♦ Why should we employ you?
♦ What are your strengths/weaknesses?
♦ Why have you stayed with your last company so long?
♦ What kind of people do you find it hard to work with?
♦ How do others see you?
♦ Where do you see yourself in three to five years?
♦ What do you do outside of work?

Another way of identifying what kind of person you are is through:

Psychometric tests
This is a psychological measurement tool used to identify your personality traits, *eg* team worker or loner, what motivates you, how well you work under pressure *etc*. This is done by asking a series of written questions and is believed to be a more scientific way of answering the question 'will you fit it?' than simply relying upon the impression created during the interview.

References
Finally, in order to ascertain other people's opinions of you, the interviewer may take up your references.

Why do you want to work here?

People like to know what prompted your application. It is also a good question to ask when trying to sift through the applicants and find out who has done their homework. Questions that could be asked include:

- Why do you want to work here?
- What do you know about the company?
- Who are our main competitors?
- What is your impression of us as a company?

How much will you work for?

This may have already been predetermined by the advert which states the salary. If not, then be prepared to negotiate. Questions may be asked such as:

- What kind of salary are you looking for?
- How much would you say you are worth?
- We can't offer the sort of money you were earning before, so how will you manage?

> **Remember, 'you don't get what you want,
> you get what you negotiate'.**

HOW WELL DO YOU KNOW YOUR CV?

We have looked at the various ways in which an interviewer will seek to gain answers to their four main questions. Although not all approaches relate specifically to your CV, it is still necessary to know your CV well, because in most cases:

> **Your CV will act as a guide and reference point for the interviewer.
> It will provide the framework and the issues for discussion.**

Therefore, for each interview, we need to be familiar with:

- which version of the CV was sent for the position being interviewed for
- dates related to the jobs we worked in
- reasons for leaving jobs
- exam results
- training taken and what we gained from it
- our hobbies and interests.

Why? Because as we are about to see in the following case study, many of the questions asked revolve around these issues.

CASE STUDIES

Brian Lynch demonstrates a positive attitude

Brian is being interviewed for a position as warehouse supervisor for a sweet manufacturer. These questions were asked:

Talk me through your career to date with British Coal.
This required Brian to be familiar with the various positions he had held. For example, his answer included: '...Having spent five years in that job, I was then promoted to supervisor.'

Brian, you spent 25 years with British Coal. Why did you leave?
As Brian's colliery was closed, he needs to answer this question positively and briefly:

'Well, my position was made redundant due to the closure of the colliery.'

Notice that Brian refers to the position being made redundant, not him.

Your CV states you were awarded a Deputy's Certificate.
What is this and what was involved in the training?

Brian needs to communicate in jargon-free language what this course was about and to emphasise what is relevant to the position applied for. For example, '... I successfully completed a supervisor's course related to health and safety and management skills.'

I notice from your hobbies and interest that you have an interest in computers. Tell me more about this.
Brian has only recently developed an interest in computers since he bought his son one. He hardly considers himself competent at this stage: '...Well, as my son wanted one for his school work, I decided it was about time I learnt about them. I'm still a beginner, but I seem to be learning new things every day.'

Brian did not use computers in his day to day work previously, but he will be required to use them if he gets the job of warehouse supervisor. The interviewer's main concerns about Brian's lack of computer experience have been alleviated to a degree because of his expressed interest. He has demonstrated a positive attitude and his ability to learn new skills quickly with the phrase: '...I seem to be learning new things every day.'

Clare Griffiths is well prepared
Clare has applied for and gained an interview for a position in an estate agency. The job appeals to her, as no previous experience is essential, although a background in sales would be preferable. Her

CV, which we saw in Chapter 4, has highlighted her communication skills and ability to deal with a wide range of people.

Why do you believe you can do this job?
The interviewer already has this information from Clare's CV and covering letter. However, the interviewer is giving Clare an opportunity to 'bring alive' this information. The interviewer knows Clare can communicate effectively in written form and is providing the opportunity to demonstrate she can do so orally.

Why did you choose banking the first place?
Clare needs to review why she chose this career before the interview. The interviewer, based on the information in Clare's CV, is giving her the opportunity to talk about herself. The CV is acting as the framework for the discussion.

After eight years away from the workplace, how will you adapt to starting a new job?
Clare's CV has highlighted her career history and therefore the dates have indicated when she was last in paid employment. The interviewer is taking his cue from Clare's CV as to the questions to ask.

By reviewing her CV beforehand and asking herself, 'if I was given this CV what questions would I want to ask', Clare could prepare herself for possible questions.

CONVINCING THE INTERVIEWER YOU'RE TELLING THE TRUTH

Your CV and covering letter have opened the door and you have an interview. You can already conclude that they like what they see and want to know more.

By asking you for an interview, the interviewer is likely to have a number of questions that need satisfying:

- Is this person as good as their CV indicates?
- Are they able to expand on the information in their CV?
- Can they back up statements of achievements?
- How well will they come across during a 'face to face'?
- Can I see this person doing the job?
- What is their appearance like?
- Am I convinced they are telling the truth?
- Can they well me more about what is not included in their CV (*eg* family details, reasons for leaving a job)?

The last thing we want to do is create one impression with our CV and then a completely different one at the interview.

How can we avoid this happening?

Firstly, when we write our CV, it should be:

- accurate
- truthful.

And just as important

- written by ourselves.

Although we may receive some help in writing our CV, ultimately it is **our** document, that advertises **us**. If we are not careful, someone else writing it for us could:

- distort the truth
- 'oversell' us
- use inappropriate language we are not comfortable with.

Remember, it is **you** who has to attend the interview, not the CV writer!

Ask for help and advice, but remember, it is important that you are able to answer the following:

- Can I justify every word on this CV?
- Is this a fair reflection of me?
- Am I comfortable with the language used?

As previously mentioned, at times we may have a tendency to undersell ourselves. That is why it is helpful to get the input of others. But beware of going from one extreme to another, from 'I am worthless and hopeless. I can't do anything' to 'I am perfect. How come this company has survived so long without me?'

Once you have completed your CV, go through each statement and make sure you are able to do the following:

Give specific and if possible, recent examples to back up each statement.

- Produce any evidence, *eg* certificates and testimonials, as validation.

If you are able to justify your statements, you achieve the following:

- You show you prepared thoroughly.
- The interviewer is likely to be convinced that you are telling the truth.

By giving examples and evidence, you make the statements on your CV create the following impression on the interviewer. They are both believable and memorable.

CASE STUDIES

Joanne Taylor is asked about her profile

Joanne has an interview for a graduate management position with large food retailer. Her interview has gone well, but now her profile is coming under the interviewer's microscope. Here are some of the questions she was asked about statements in her profile.

- 'Joanne, you state in your profile that you are able to motivate others. Can you give me an example of when you last did this?'

- 'You describe yourself as being as excellent communicator. Define communication and what makes you excellent at doing it.'

- 'You believe you possess effective problem solving skills. Convince me that you have.'

The interviewer has every right to ask these questions. If Joanne believes she has these abilities and has said so on her CV, then she must be prepared to back them up. If she is not able to answer convincingly, the interviewer is left wondering.

- Is she telling the truth?
- Has she just 'dried up'?
- Did someone else write this CV for her?

An interviewer is unlikely to take everything you say on your CV at face value. Be prepared for them to dig beneath the surface.

Colin Burrows registers with an agency

Colin has applied for a variety of jobs without gaining an interview. It is realistic to conclude that however effective your CV is, there may be a number of reasons why you are not obtaining interviews.

◆ You may be too old/young.
◆ Someone else had more relevant experience.
◆ You were based in the wrong location.
◆ Someone else was already in line for the job.
◆ Any others?

Colin, faced with a series of rejection letters, has therefore registered with an agency. We saw his covering letter in Chapter 5. He was asked by his interviewer:

◆ Convince me that you are prepared to take a drop in salary.

◆ Define 'within reasonable driving distance from Warrington' to me.

◆ Why have you never stayed in one job longer than five years?

◆ What would you not want a company to know about you?

Colin has been asked a number of difficult questions by the interviewer from the agency. Why? The agency may have a number of positions Colin may be suitable for. How Colin answers these questions will help clarify in their minds what kind of person he is and how he copes under pressure. The agency is doing Colin a favour by asking such questions; it is good preparation for future interviews. Remember also that this may only be an interview with an agency, but Colin still has to sell himself. The agency may want to present a shortlist of suitable candidates to their client. In order to maintain their own reputation, it is important that the agency submits credible candidates.

Colin's CV and covering letter were the focal point for his discussion with the agency. Prior preparation will help Colin deal confidently with questions asked. In order to help Colin's preparation and your own, ask yourself:

♦ What questions would I want to ask, if I was reading this CV for the first time?

ACTION AND REFLECTION

Action points

1 There are different types of interview. They may take place face to face or over the phone.
2 Whatever type of interview, preparation is vital.
3 Review the four key areas the interviewers want to satisfy in their own minds.
4 What is on your CV will in most cases be the focal point of the interview. Therefore, make sure you know your CV.
5 We must be prepared to back up and justify everything on our CV. Prepare examples and bring testimonials and certificates if necessary.

Points to consider

♦ What feelings do people typically experience when preparing for interview?
♦ What is it about an interview that generates these feelings?
♦ What is the worst thing that can happen at an interview?
♦ Why is putting the interview into perspective so important?

8

Some Final Thoughts

DISCOVER THE VITAL INGREDIENT OF SUCCESS – ATTITUDE

Looking for work or seeking to gain new business is not easy. As we have seen, in many ways it is important to see yourself as a salesperson and one thing salespeople have to get used to is **rejection**.

You are now in a position to write a winning CV that presents you in the best and most appropriate light. Yet despite this, you are still likely to face rejection. When this happens self esteem can take a knock and it soon becomes easy to give up.

Remember though, the only difference between winners and losers is this:

> **Winners and losers both get knocked down,**
> **but only losers stay down.**

Attitude will play a vital part in your success, specifically in relation to:

♦ how you see yourself
♦ how you see your future.

This book has given you insights into yourself by helping you to:

♦ identify your skills
♦ highlight your achievements
♦ market yourself through your CV.

As we have discussed, the world of work is changing and we must be prepared to do the same. In order to do so, we must be positive in our attitude and remember there are always two ways of looking at things.

Negative thinking	Positive thinking
1 in 10 people are out of work.	9 out of 10 are in work.
I am fast approaching 40.	I have another 25 years to offer an employer.
I've had a number of jobs.	I've gained valuable experience in a variety of positions.
I have only worked for one company.	I've demonstrated a successful track record, I am reliable and dependable and not a job hopper.
I failed at my interview.	I gained valuable experience which will help me in the future.

Fig. 17. Postive and negative thinking.

How we **think** will determine how we **act**, as will our belief about ourselves and our future.

A negative attitude can lead to a self-fulfilling prophecy and so can a positive one.

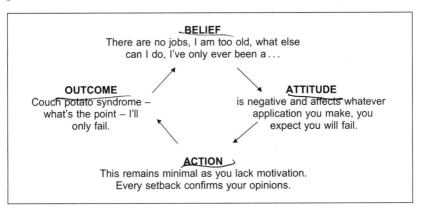

Fig. 18. The self-fulfilling prophecy.

PUTTING YOUR CV TO WORK

It is not enough to simply be positive. Being positive alone will not lead to success. We must take action!

Many of my clients have found using a personal action plan helpful. It helps in the following ways:

+ It focuses your attention.
+ It helps organise your activity.
+ It acts as a record.
+ It provides discipline and structure.

You can devise your own plan which should include:

+ people to contact
+ research to undertake
+ letters to write
+ places to visit
+ follow up of previous action
+ telephone calls to make.

It is important not just to have a winning CV, but to put it to work to your advantage. An action plan would normally include:

What I am going to do	How I am going to do it	When I am going to do it by

Fig 19. Action plan.

ADAPTING TO THE CHANGING TIMES

The world of work has dramatically changed over the last 15 years. The two main contributing factors are:

◆ recession of the early 1990s plus the financial global crisis in 2008
◆ technological advances.

The recession of the early 1990s led to the following:

◆ Companies are less willing to commit themselves to offering permanent jobs. This has resulted in an increase in:
  – temporary work (recruiting through agencies)
  – fixed term contracts
  – part-time work
  – work being contracted out to consultants.

◆ Organisations were forced to examine their company structures in order to become more competitive. This has led to a move away from hierarchical organisations to ones of a 'flatter' nature.

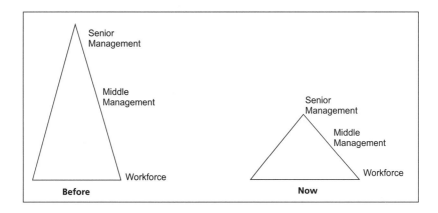

Fig. 20. Changes in organisational structures.

Technological advances

These have also meant fewer people are now required to do the work and, as communication has advanced, people are increasingly likely to work from home.

How this affects you

- You may have been a victim of the company reorganisation and that is why you are reading this book!

- Technological advances may have meant your skills were obsolete and your services were not required.

- Your company may still have required your services, but as a 'contractor' and not as an employee, therefore forcing you into self-employment.

- Because there are fewer layers to climb within an organisation, you may be seeking fresh challenges elsewhere in order to advance your career.

- Fewer jobs have led to fierce competition, particularly amongst school leavers and graduates.

HOW TO RESPOND TO CHANGE

We have already seen the importance of attitude and our own outlook must take these changes into account.

We must be...

Flexible

Be prepared to change with the times rather than resisting them.

Adaptable

We must adapt and develop our skills to needs of the market.

Education must be seen as an ongoing process no matter what your age. People must be prepared to learn new skills.

Risk takers
There is no guarantee of a 'job for life' any more. We must be prepared to work on a self employed basis.

Long term in our outlook
Walking into the job of our dreams is unlikely to happen for most of us. We must be prepared to study or to do voluntary work in order to gain experience and new skills, even if the 'pay off' is not immediate. We must see some jobs as stepping stones to something better.

Realistic in our expectations
If we are changing careers, we may have to accept a lower salary. If we are starting a business, we need to give it time to grow. If we have qualifications but little experience, we must be prepared to start at a lower level in order to acquire experience.

Positive
Change is easier to accept when we are positive about it. We need to see these changes as opportunities, not as problems.

Sales people
That's where your CV comes in! Whatever skills or experience we have, we still need to sell ourselves. This is an attitude that should encompass not only our CV but all aspects of our job search or business development.

> 'The future does not belong to the strongest,
> but to those who are best able to adapt to change.'
> **Charles Darwin**

THE CV AS A 'PICK-ME-UP'

We have seen how facing rejection is almost a prerequisite for achieving success. How can we come to terms with this? The best antidote to depression is action. Implementing our action plan will make us feel better, because:

Right feelings follow right actions.

There are two responses to rejection:

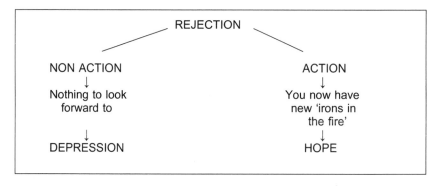

Fig 21. Responses to rejection.

Review your CV

In order to further lift your spirits, review your CV. By now, you have developed your own sales brochure. You have recalled achievements, identified your skills and been equipped with the knowledge of how to market yourself successfully.

But now indulge yourself for a moment. Do not simply be aware of what is on your CV but:

◆ Re-live those achievements in your mind.

◆ Focus on the skills you have and imagine using them in a variety of situations.

◆ Congratulate yourself and be thankful for the education and training you have received, whether you gained any qualifications or not.

◆ Say to yourself 'this is me . . .' as you read your profile.

And then **take action**. Your self indulgence is over, it's time to start implementing your action plan and take personal responsibility for your future.

DEVELOPING YOUR DYNAMIC DOCUMENT

A CV is never complete until you die. The need for a CV may decrease during your career, but it is never complete. Many people simply 'update' their CV when they change jobs. Be prepared to do more than that.

◆ As you change, so should your CV. Is it still a fair reflection of who you are now or does it still reflect where you were when it was first written?

◆ Have you re-analysed the skills you possess and included new ones you have acquired?

◆ What about your personal attributes? Has there been a change of emphasis? Do you still feel comfortable and able to justify your statements?

Remember, your CV encapsulates **you**:

♦ Who **you** are.

♦ What **you** have done.

♦ What skills **you** possess.

♦ What **you** have achieved.

Your CV reflects your life to date in a condensed form. Although its main purpose is to inform others about you, it also helps provide you with a personal insight. By reviewing and reflecting on your CV, you can assess not just what you have done, but what you might do in the future.

Your CV is much more than just an academic exercise to complete. As long as you change, so will your CV. For this reason, it is a dynamic document.

CASE STUDIES

Clare Griffiths highlights action points

What am I going to do?	How am I going to do it?	When am I going to do it by?
1. Contact Janice, Linda and Stephanie (ex bank colleagues)	Telephone	Week ending 10/12
2. Speak to Beryl (mobile hairdresser)	When she next visits	Week ending 9/1
3. Contact local college re word processing course	Ring for prospectus	Week ending 10/12
4. Contact Vivian Johnson (parent governor) to act as a referee	Write a letter	Week ending 18/1
5. Have 30 copies of CV produced	Ask Bob to get them printed at his work	Week ending 10/12
6. Research on-line job agencies	Via the Internet	Week ending 10/12

Clare has highlighted six action points to take. These including contacting:

◆ ex colleagues
◆ those she comes into contact with on a regular basis (mobile hairdresser, parent governor).

Also she will need plenty of copies of her CV which she is arranging to have printed at her husband's work. Her skills analysis identified a training need in the area of word processing and basic computer skills. This she intends to address by starting the appropriate course at her local college. She is also going to find out about on-line job agencies by searching the Internet at a local cyber-café.

Colin Burrows highlights action points

What am I going to do?	How am I going to do it?	When am I going to do it by?
1. Contact my local Learning and Skills Council	Ring to make an appointment	Week ending 9/1
2. Contact career guidance regarding taking a psychometric test	Ring to make an appointment	Week ending 9/1
3. Contact agencies	Send CVs and follow up with a phone call	Week ending 3/12
4. Contact Paul Jennings (businessman)	Invite him round for a meal	Week ending 3/12
5. Identify companies to contact on a speculative basis	Visit reference library	Week ending 10/12
6. Contact bank manager re financial situation	Telephone and arrange an appointment	Week ending 3/12

Colin is likely to remain in accountancy, but still wants to explore other options. Some of his activity is therefore focused on:

♦ retraining options
♦ careers guidance.

The local Learning and Skills Council (LSC) could provide Colin with a wealth of information concerning retraining. In order to find out exactly how they can help, he is ringing to arrange an appointment. Career Centres do not just deal with school leavers, but increasingly with a wide range of older people. Colin has a vague idea of their service, but his plan of action includes arranging an appointment with a careers adviser.

His action plan is not concentrated purely on job search and acquiring information on a change of career, but also on practical issues relating to finance. Rather than worry about what will happen to his house if he does not succeed in finding work quickly, he is arranging to see his bank manager. A 'clear the air talk' will relieve some of the stress relating to Colin's financial position.

The main conclusion to draw from Colin's action plan is **'if you don't know, find out'**.

ACTION AND SELF-ASSESSMENT

Action points

1 Because we are likely to face rejection, a positive attitude can motivate us to 'stick with it'.
2 Having a good CV is useless unless we take action and put it to work.
3 Compile our own action plan and review and update it regularly.

4 Review the points on how we must respond to the changes in the world of work. Which is most necessary for you to do?

5 The CV is a reflection of the 'real you', so use it as a 'pick-me-up' whenever you face setbacks.

6 Your CV is a dynamic document that changes and develops as you do.

Self-assessment

♦ What have been the main points you have learned from this book?

♦ How would you describe yourself? Naturally optimistic or pessimistic?

♦ How do you feel about change? Resigned to it, or excited by it?

♦ Having read this book, how would you now describe your feelings about yourself and your future?

More Sample Covering Letters

COVERING LETTER – STRAIGHT AND TO THE POINT

Mrs P Jackson
Credit Control Manager
Newsquest Ltd
The Academy
93 Brown Street
Altrincham
Cheshire
WA17 9FP

Lisa Ackroyd
74 Osborne Street
Atrincham
Cheshire
WA17 2PB

24th July 20XX

Dear Mrs Jackson

Credit Control Administration Clerk

Please find enclosed my CV in connection with the above position. As you will see from my CV, I am experienced in Microsoft Excel and Word, having used both packages in my current position. I have excellent keyboard skills and am used to working unsupervised, prioritising my own workload.

I believe I have a great deal to bring to this position and am particularly excited about the prospect of working in such a dynamic industry such as news.

I look forward to hearing from you.

Yours sincerely

Lisa Ackroyd

DETAILED COVERING LETTER

> Gail Roberts
> 15 Linden Close
> Renforth Marsh
> Newcastle
> NE12 3LN
>
> Dear Mrs Merrett
>
> Please find enclosed my application for the position of Staff Nurse at Wheatfields Childrens Hospice. In addition, I would like to add the following in support of my application.
>
> During my nursing training I spent a significant amount of time working with sick children and always found it rewarding and fulfilling. I have found it crucial to build rapport with the children's parents, siblings and other staff in my work and believe my openness and ability to empathize is my greatest asset. In addition, I feel comfortable relating to people of all ages. I possess a good sense of humour and am well organised. From a personal perspective, I consider my life to be 'rich' and this would help me to enable the sick children to enjoy living despite the inevitable outcome of their condition.
>
> Working as a team is, I believe, vital in providing care and I have also enjoyed this aspect of my work, as well as being able to work on my own initiative. I believe I possess the necessary qualities and attributes that this post demands and look forward to the opportunity of contributing to this vitally important work.
>
> Yours sincerely
>
> Gail Roberts

Another Sample CV

JAMES HART
59 Carrington Lane
Bradley
Bristol
BR25 4MP
Tel: 01406 9537762

PROFILE

An adaptable, enthusiastic, conscientious and self-motivated individual with broad ranging experience. Possessing excellent communication skills combined with the ability to relate well to people at all levels and ensuring jobs are seen through from conception to successful completion.

CAREER SKILLS AND ACHIEVEMENTS

Estimating/Systems Development

- Running a daily cost estimating system providing performance and costing data using a wide variety of software packages.
- Producing daily, weekly, monthly, quarterly and yearly reports drawn from production data.
- Part of a forecasting and scheduling team, producing recommendations in the form of reports to the sales and management team.

Production – Team Leader

- Supervised a team of 20 staff on a shift rota basis and ensured that production targets and quality standards were consistently met in a hazardous environment, where safety and hygiene were paramount.
- Dealt with all personnel matters relating to the team including their training, development, sickness and holiday cover.

- Increased production by 30% through new working practices, improved operating systems, better team understanding and working methods.
- Implemented perpetual product inventory (PPI), which improved the measurement of stock from delivery to end product and subsequently this reduced stockholding and related costs.

Customer Service
- Dealt with a broad range of customers' needs and requirements on a fast-moving and dynamic shipping line, requiring good communication, organisation and excellent interpersonal skills.

Warehouse Operative
- Duties included: Picking, Packing, QA, International Despatch, System Interrogation. Fully trained on 'Dispatcher' Warehouse Management System.

TECHNICAL SKILLS

Word Processing:	Microsoft Word 2003
	WordPerfect – v7.0 for Windows
Spreadsheet Software:	Lotus 123 for Windows (Advanced)
	Microsoft Excel 2003
Presentation Software:	Harvard Graphics
Email Software:	Lotus CCMAIL
	Lotus Notes
Other Software:	Corel Flow
	MS Office
	Dispatcher (Warehouse Management System)

CAREER SUMMARY

1999 – Present	Estimator/Systems Development Technician, Molvane Cellular Accessories
1997 – 1999	Team Leader – Operations, Wellington International, Bath
1997	Despatch Clerk, Leaf (UK) Ltd, Bristol
1995 – 1997	Cabin Supervisor, Stena Line (UK) Ltd, Holyhead, North Wales

EDUCATION AND TRAINING

BA(Hons) in Leisure Studies
HND in Leisure Studies
National Diploma in Business and Computer Studies
RSA Level 2 in Information Technology
GCSEs in Maths, English, Welsh Studies and Science

Attended a number of courses in a variety of computer software packaging, other training included:

Selling Skills
Basic Food Hygiene
Sea Safety
Accident Reporting
Efficient Deck Hand (EDH)

PERSONAL DETAILS

Date of Birth: 9 May 1974
Marital Status: Married
Full clean driving licence, car owner

LEISURE INTERESTS

In my leisure time I enjoy playing rugby. Whilst at university, I represented Bedfordshire and East Midlands Colt and U21s teams. For seven years I was in the Air Training Corps where I reached the rank of Cadet Warrant Officer. My most enjoyable pastime is spending time with my family and friends.

Glossary

Agencies/recruitment consultants. Privately run businesses operating to recruit staff on behalf of other organisations.

Blue chip company. A business which is listed on the stock exchange. It is a term used to express the credibility of an organisation.

Career history. An overview of a person's career, which includes dates and the names of the organisations worked for.

Chronological CV. A CV which lists in date order the organisations worked for.

Covering letter. A letter which accompanies a CV or application form when contacting an employer.

Functional CV. A CV which gives an overview of the type of work done and skills acquired, with less emphasis on when the jobs were done and for whom.

Human resources. A term used in reference to the organisation and management of people within an organisation.

IPD. The Institute of Personnel and Development which is an amalgamation of the Institute of Personnel Management (IPM) and the Institute of Training and Development (ITD). Its members concentrate on the people management within an organisation.

IR. Industrial relations. A term used to describe the working relations between management and the workforce, usually in connection with pay and working conditions.

Job description. A list of broadly defined duties and responsibilities attached to a particular job.

K. An initial representing a thousand pounds in monetary terms, *eg* £250k is £250,000.

Learning and Skills Council (LSC). Government-funded agency responsible for providing training opportunities.

NVQ. National Vocational Qualification, which can be gained through assessment 'on the job' as opposed to studying and sitting exams.

On file. A term used by organisations who keep hold of your CV or application form for a given period, with the possibility of contacting you should a suitable vacancy arise.

OTE. On-target earnings, *ie* the amount of salary which will be paid provided certain sales or other business targets are met.

Profile. A summary of your main skills and attributes, which can be included at the beginning of a CV.

Psychometric tests. Exercises and questionnaires designed to measure a range of skills, general intelligence, personality traits and motivational drives.

Referees. Individuals who agree to provide information to a third party about a person's character. Work referees may also provide information about competence, absenteeism and punctuality.

Skills. The ability and talent to carry out a given task competently and effectively.

Speculative approach. Contact initiated by an individual to an organisation, on the chance that they may have a suitable vacancy.

Targeted CV. A CV written with a specific job in mind and tailored to emphasise the most relevant points.

Transferable skills. Abilities and talents which can be adapted or reshaped by an individual into different working situations and environments.

Work experience. The time spent in a working environment acquiring skills and knowledge of working practices.

Further Reading

Build Your Own Rainbow, Hobson and Scally, Lifeskills

Career Change, Ruth Lancashire and Roger Holdsworth, Hobsons

Going Freelance, Godfrey Golzan, Kogan Page

Great Answers to Tough Interview Questions, Yate, Kogan Page

High Powered CVs, Rachel Bishop Firth, How To Books

How to Find the Perfect Job, Tom Jackson, Piatkus

How to Get a Job After 45, Julie Bayley, Kogan Page

How to Write a Winning CV, Alan Jones, Hutchinson Business Books

The Job Application Handbook, Judith Johnstone, How To Books

Know Your Own IQ, H J Eysenck, Penguin

Know Your Own Personality, Glen Wilson and H J Eysenck, Penguin

Passing That Interview, Judith Johnstone, How To Books

Returning to Work, Alex Reed, Kogan Page

Shut Up, Move On, Paul McGee, Capstone

Start and Run a Profitable Consulting Business, Douglas A Gray, Kogan Page

What Colour Is Your Parachute?, Richard Bolles, Ten Speed Press

Where to Find That Job, Alan Bartlett, Hobsons

Useful Addresses

Alliance of Small Firms and Self Employed People, 33 The Green, Calne, Wiltshire SN11 8DJ

Careers Research and Advisory Centre (CRAC), Bateman Street, Cambridge CB2 1LZ

CEPEC Recruitment Guide, CEPEC Publications, Kent House, 41 East Street, Bromley, Kent BR1 1QC

Learning and Skills Council helpline: 0870 9006800

National Advisory Centre on Careers for Women, Drayton House, 30 Gordon Street, London WC1M 0AX

National Institute of Adult Continuing Education (NIACE), 9b De Montfort Street, Leicester LE1 7GE. Tel: (01533) 551451

Paul McGee Associates, 20 Delphfields Road, Appleton, Warrington, Cheshire WA4 5BY. Website: *www.paulmcgee.com*

The Career Changers Network of Women in Management, 64 Marryat Road, London SW19 5BN

The Executive Grapevine, Executive Grapevine Ltd, 79 Manor Way, Blackheath, London SE3 9XG

The Open College, FREEPOST, PO Box 35, Abingdon, Oxfordshire OX14 3BB

The National Council for Voluntary Organisations, 26 Bedford Square, London WC1B 3HV

Open University, Student Enquiries Office, PO Box 71, Milton Keynes MK7 6AG

Voluntary Services Overseas (VSO), 9 Belgrave Square, London SW1X 8PW

Useful Website Addresses

www.learntheinternet.com
www.monster.co.uk
www.totaljobs.com
www.fish4jobs.co.uk
www.topjobs.net
www.thejob.com
www.europages.com

Index

HOW TO WRITE AN IMPRESSIVE CV & COVER LETTER
A comprehensive guide for the UK job seeker
TRACEY WHITMORE

Includes a free CD with templates and real-life examples

Your CV and cover letter are your first communication with a prospective employer. As the job market has become increasingly competitive, making the right first impression has never been more important. If you compromise on the quality of your CV and cover letter, you greatly reduce your chances of winning an interview.

This book, which will appeal to anyone from entry level to board level, encompasses a step-by-step guide on how to achieve killer competitive advantage by producing a thoroughly impressive CV and cover letter. The job acquisition process, which has changed significantly in recent years, is discussed fully, and really effective job-hunting tactics are provided.

- ◆ Interviews undertaken with top HR professionals, who are often the first point of entry, outline what you need to do to impress them. Their views and opinions are provided throughout the book.

- ◆ The book and CD are packed with practical examples of CVs and cover letters that have actually worked in real-life. These individuals were struggling to win interviews prior to their CV revamp. Their new CVs secured several interviews, many of which resulted in job offers.

- ◆ The CD contains CV and cover letter templates, and full transcripts of interviews held with twelve industry experts from blue chip employers such as Vodafone, Tesco, KPMG, Korn Ferry and Jonathan Wren.

ISBN 978-1-84528-365-0

WHY SHOULD I WORK FOR YOU?
How to find the job that's right for you – and get the offer
KEITH POTTS AND JASON DEIGN

This book starts from the premise that in today's uncertain job market you, not your employer, call the shots in your career. Packed with tips, exercises and case studies, it will give you all you need to create a 'you-shaped job' and set the course for a better life. Discover: the four things you need to get any job; a unique way of working out which job you should be doing; six ways to get more money out of your current employer even if they won't give you a pay rise; how to avoid pitfalls in job hunting and interviews; how to create a life-long plan that will help you enjoy a happy and fulfilling career for the rest of your working days. Author, Keith Potts is an acknowledged expert on employment practices and trends as a result of his role as founder and managing director of Jobsite UK, one of the UK's leading commercial Internet recruitment services.

ISBN 978-1-84528-347-6

HANDLING TOUGH JOB INTERVIEWS
JULIE-ANN AMOS

'This book aims to prepare you for anything in job interviews, whether by a recruitment agency, headhunter, employer or human resources department.' – *Ms London Weekly*

'It covers all kinds of interview from recruitment agencies and headhunters to employer and human resources.' *Phoenix*

'The book gives a wealth of sound advice, including good hints on how to make the right impression, the best questions to ask, how to approach negotiating a salary, taking a psychometric test and how you should treat a regular interview differently from one with a recruitment agency or a head-hunter.' *Sesame, Open University Magazine*

ISBN 978-1-84528-358-2

HOW TO ANSWER HARD INTERVIEW QUESTIONS
CHARLIE GIBBS

'Allows us to actually get inside the head of an interviewer and explore in detail the hundreds of questions he or she may pose to us on the day. Written in a no-nonsense conversational style this book covers everything you need to know about an interview – before, during and after the interview.' *www.streetbrand.com*

As well as tips on how to prepare for, and conduct yourself at the interview itself, this book has examples of the kind of answers interviewers really want to hear; the kind of answers that will get you that job. And if you can't find the answer to the question you want the author invites you to email it to him and he'll send an answer!

ISBN 978-1-84528-238-7

PASSING PSYCHOMETRIC TESTS
ANDREA SHAVICK

'A very good aid for those who might find themselves facing a psychometric questionnaire.' – *Irish Examiner*

'...an insightful book.' – *The Guardian*

ISBN 978-1-84528-222-6

HOW TO SUCCEED AT INTERVIEWS
DR ROB YEUNG

'To be interviewed without having read it is an opportunity missed.' – *Sunday Times*

'*How To Succeed at Interviews* is the type of book that one may not wish to share with others who are job seeking in competition with oneself.' *S Lewis, Coventry*

'... an invaluable source of information for job hunters on preparing for interviews, tests and assessment centres.' – *Jonathan Turpin, Chief Executive, fish4jobs.co.uk*

'This is an excellent book; good value ... buy it.' – *V Tilbury, Cranfield University*

'An engaging read packed with useful observations and tips for job seekers of all ages.' – *Roddy Gow, Chairman, Odgers, Ray & Berndtson*

ISBN 978-1-84528-259-2

PSYCHOMETRIC TESTS FOR GRADUATES
ANDREA SHAVICK

This book contains 37 genuine graduate-level practice tests from SHL Group plc, the biggest test publisher in the world; 227 questions covering verbal, numerical, abstract and spatial reasoning, mechanical comprehension, fault diagnosis, accuracy and personality; and genuine practice *Brainstorm, Scenarios* and *Fastrack* management tests.

ISBN 978-1-84528-262-2

PRACTICE PSYCHOMETRIC TESTS
ANDREA SHAVICK

This book is crammed full of even more genuine practice psychometric tests from SHL Group plc, the biggest test publisher in the world. It contains 334 questions covering verbal, numerical, abstract and spatial reasoning, mechanical comprehension, fault diagnosis, accuracy and personality, including the popular *OPQ 32* personality questionnaire.

ISBN 978-1-84528-020-8

MANAGEMENT-LEVEL PSYCHOMETRIC AND ASSESSMENT CENTRE TESTS
ANDREA SHAVICK

Whether you're after a junior management, senior management or even director-level position, or simply want to familiarise yourself with the very latest selection and recruitment techniques, you need this book!

ISBN 978-1-84528-028-4

IMPROVE YOUR PUNCTUATION AND GRAMMAR
MARION FIELD

'Invaluable guide...after reading this book, you will never again find yourself using a comma instead of a semi-colon.' – *Evening Standard*

'I can't recommend this book highly enough. Every writer should have a copy.' – *Writers' Bulletin*

ISBN 978-1-84528-329-2

IMPROVE YOUR WRITTEN ENGLISH
MARION FIELD

'If your written English is letting you down, do something about it. This book is recommended.' – *Evening Standard*

'This book is a gem. If you never buy another reference book, buy this one!' – *Writers' Express*

ISBN 978-1-84528-331-5

QUICK SOLUTIONS TO COMMON ERRORS IN ENGLISH
ANGELA BURT

'With this A-Z guide to spelling, punctuation and grammar
you will never doubt your written English again.' – *Evening Standard*

'A very useful tool...could easily fill that hole on your bookshelf.' – *Irish Independent*

'...straightforward and accessible handbook for anyone who ever has a
query about correct English – and that's all of us.' – *Freelance News*

ISBN 978-1-84528-361-2

How To Books are available through all good bookshops, or you can order direct from us through Grantham Book Services.
Tel: +44 (0)1476 541080
Fax: +44 (0)1476 541061
Email: orders@gbs.tbs-ltd.co.uk

Or via our website

www.howtobooks.co.uk

To order via any of these methods please quote the title(s) of the book(s) and your credit card number together with its expiry date.

For further information about our books and catalogue, please contact:

How To Books
Spring Hill House
Spring Hill Road
Begbroke
Oxford OX5 1RX

Visit our web site at www.howtobooks.co.uk

Or you can contact us by email at info@howtobooks.co.uk